WITHDRAWAL

ORA WILLIAMS

American Black Women
in the Arts and Social Sciences:

A Bibliographic Survey

Revised and expanded edition

by

ORA WILLIAMS

The Scarecrow Press, Inc.
Metuchen, N.J. & London
1978

Library of Congress Cataloging in Publication Data

Williams, Ora, 1926-
    American Black women in the arts and social sciences.

    Includes index.
    1. Afro-American women--Bibliography. I. Title.
Z1361.N39W56   1977   [E185.86]   016.3014'12'0922
ISBN 0-8108-1096-4   77-17055

The "beautyful" ones have been born:

My parents, Charles and Ida Williams; my sister,
Martha Blanche Williams Wright; my brother, Charles
Williams; and the incomparable Fannie Lou Hamer.

TABLE OF CONTENTS

PREFACE

In 1971, when I began my research on works created by American Black women, little of a positive nature was available. So little emphasis was being placed on positive contributions of American Black women that teachers of women's courses were constantly asking me for the name of a Black woman poet, dramatist, or novelist. Moreover, students enrolled in classes about Black women readily admitted that they could not cite the names and contributions of notable American Black women in any areas other than the field of popular entertainment. Much has changed since that period, however, and a number of excellent references on Black women exclusively, and others which include contributions of Black women, have appeared. The works of American Black women are more readily accessible in the market place than they were in 1971.

Although some strides have been made and although Black women have produced and continue to produce more works in the arts and social sciences than anyone can hope to index completely, there is still great reluctance to recognize the humanity of American Black women. Despite the widespread consciousness-raising activities of feminists and Black civil rights advocates, there is an overwhelming failure to transfer the new awareness to Black women. In fact, for these rights groups too, Black women remain, as Zora Neale Hurston said, the mules of the world. There is, far too often, little difference between the treatment Black women receive from overt racists and that which they receive from many ardent feminists or Black males. Both categories appear to find it too threatening or an imposition to be exposed to Black women's points of view or aspects of the "double and triple indemnity." And, naturally, being relegated to the place of a mule is, as one would expect, beginning to have a tragic and obvious effect on American Black women.

The purposes of this work are many. It should have a regenerating effect on Black women. It should make it unmistakably clear that thousands more than our beloved and distinguished two--Sojourner Truth and Harriet Tubman-- have rendered and are rendering unparalleled contributions through the arts, social sciences, visions, and good deeds. In addition to projecting some of the great wealth and diversity of talent among Black women, this book seeks to provide students with resources that will assist them in their research, and it celebrates many unsung heroines--our foremothers, sisters, and daughters--in the spirit which pervades Jewell Handy Gresham's tribute on the death of her mother who, like many of our mothers, left behind a legacy rich in the qualities of fortitude and humanistic dedication which distinguished the worthiest of womankind, of mankind:

Poem for Mama Essie*

What strength from your dauntless Soul
Transmutes our grief into quiet.
The beauty of your spirit

---

*Mama Essie refers to Mrs. Essie Jones Handy, School Teacher, Community Leader, and Civil Libertarian, who resided in Lafayette, Alabama, from 1925 until her death in 1977.

Glows luminously in the stillness
Of Life passing into Afterlife
And Peace.
Yours, the quick darting personality
Expanding into character;
Character, unquenchable
Lifted to dimensions;
Dimensions, unlimited
Soaring into horizons
Framing worlds before us
Unending.
Now, in the distance
Your gallant figure recedes
Into infinity--into oneness
With Nature and Immortality.
With Love, enduring...
Forever.

Jewell Handy Gresham

Many revisions were made in this edition of American Black Women. Hundreds of additional titles appear here.
Some sections have been merged, and some have been de-
leted. A list of significant dates and a list of some important ideas and achievements of Black women appear. Some
recordings of Black women artists whose talents tend to be
ignored are listed. In addition, photographs of art work and
of artists and authors are included.

With the exception of some works in the sections
"Bibliographies and Guides to Collections," "Encyclopedias,
Handbooks, and Other Reference Books," "Biography and
Criticism by Authors Other Than Black Women," "Non-Black
Women Editors," and the "Biography and Criticism" sub-
sections of "Selected Individual Bibliography," all other ref-
erences in this work are by Black women. The intention is
to highlight the talents of American Black women.

CHRONOLOGY

Some Significant Dates in the History
of American Black Women

1619   The first Black slaves landed at Jamestown Harbor, Virginia.

1746   Lucy Terry, whose poem "Bars of Flight" appeared in this year, was the first Black American to have a poem published.

1770   Phillis Wheatley's poem "An Elegiac Poem on the Death of the Rev'd Mr. George Whitefield--1770" was published.

1780   Massachusetts declared all men to be born free and equal.

1783   The second published volume of poetry by an American woman and the first volume of poetry by an American Black person was Phillis Wheatley's Poems on Various Subjects, Religious and Moral.

1786   The New York African Free School was begun.

1790   All Blacks in Boston, Massachusetts, were freed.

1797   Sojourner Truth is said to have been born around this time in Ulster County, New York.

1816   The first independent Black church, the African Methodist Episcopal Church, was founded in Philadelphia.

1820   This date is the approximate birthdate of Harriet Tubman, Eastern Shore, Maryland.

1821   The African Grove Theater, the first Black theatrical company, was organized in New York City.

1827   Sojourner Truth won her freedom.

1831   The first convention of "people of color" met in Philadelphia.

1837   The American Friends founded the Institute for Colored Youth in Philadelphia.

A national convention of Negro women met in Philadelphia to promote the abolition of slavery.

1848   William and Mary Ellen Craft escaped from slavery.

1849   Harriet Tubman escaped from slavery in Maryland.

1850   Lucy Sessions earned a degree from Oberlin, possibly becoming the first Black woman in America to receive a college degree.

The Narrative of Sojourner Truth as told to Olive Gilbert appeared.

1853   Rachel Parker, who won her freedom in a Maryland state court, is thought to have been the first Black freed by a slave state court.

1854   Poems on Miscellaneous Subjects, by Frances Harper, was published.

Elizabeth Greenfield, also known as "The Black Swan," gave a command performance at Buckingham Palace for Queen Victoria.

1856   Wilberforce College was founded by the African Methodist Episcopal Church.

1862   Harriet Tubman served as a spy, scout, and guerrilla leader for the Union Army.

1864   Fannie Jackson Coppin was one of forty students selected to teach preparatory classes at Oberlin.

Mary Ellen Pleasant, civil rights advocate and abolitionist, sued the San Francisco Street Car Company for rude treatment given her and two other Black women.

Sojourner Truth was appointed counselor to freed Blacks in Arlington Heights, Virginia.

Edmonia Lewis, first American Negro woman sculptor to achieve distinction in this field, exhibited her work in Boston.

1866   Fisk University opened in Nashville, Tennessee.

1867   Howard University was established in Washington, D. C.

1868   Hampton Institute was established in Hampton, Virginia.

1871   Edmonia Lewis received acclaim in Rome for her exhibit of sculpture.

Sarah Parker Redmond, abolitionist and medical doctor, earned her medical degree from a medical school in Florence, Italy.

1872   Biddy Mason, pioneer, laundry woman, philanthropist, was one of the founders of the first Black church in Los Angeles, the First A. M. E. Church.

1876   Edmonia Lewis exhibited her sculpture, "Death of Cleopatra," in the Centennial Celebration, Philadelphia.

1884   Ida B. Wells sued the Chesapeake and Ohio Railroad Company for assault.

The African Methodist Episcopal Church Review was established.

1886   Lucy Laney founded Haines Institute in Augusta, Georgia.

The Alpha Home for Aged Colored Women, perhaps the first of its kind, was opened in Indiana.

1889   Ida B. Wells, one of the first Black newspaper women, became one of the editors of the Memphis Free Speech and Headlight.

Emma Azalia Hackley, author, composer, performer,

teacher, was graduated from the College of Music, Denver, Colorado.

1892   Frances Harper, abolitionist, feminist, lecturer, poet, became the first Black woman to publish a novel, Iola Leroy or Shadows Uplifted.

1893   Ida B. Wells expanded her anti-lynching crusade with a lecture tour in England.

1895   Black women from twenty Black women's clubs formed the National Federation of Afro-American Women.

1896   The National League of Colored Women and the National Federation of Afro-American Women joined, becoming the National Association of Colored Women (NACW).

1897   Dr. Matilda Arabelle Evans was graduated from Women's Medical College in Pennsylvania.

Victoria Earle Matthews, author and teacher, founded the White Rose Home Mission in New York City, similar to the Travelers' Aid Society, but for Black women.

1898   Ida B. Wells led a group of women and congressmen to discuss with President William McKinley the lynching of a Black postmaster.

1902   Charlotte Hawkins Brown founded Palmer Institute in Sedalia, North Carolina.

1903   Maggie L. Walker opened the St. Luke Penny Savings Bank in Richmond, Virginia, becoming the first woman bank president in the United States.

1904   Mary McLeod Bethune founded the Daytona Educational and Industrial Training School, later known as Bethune-Cookman College.

Mary Church Terrell addressed the Geneva International Congress of Women in Berlin, speaking in several languages.

1905   Eva Bowles accepted a position at the Harlem Branch

of the YWCA, becoming the first Black woman on the
YWCA staff.

Madame C. J. Walker invented the straightening
comb.

1908   Janie Barrett was made president of the newly-formed
        Virginia State Federation of Women.

        Alpha Kappa Alpha Sorority was founded at Howard
        University, Washington, D. C.

1909   Nannie Burroughs founded the National Training
        School for Women, Washington, D. C.

1912   Charlotta (Spears) Bass, civil rights fighter and poli-
        tician, became the owner, editor, and publisher of
        The Eagle (The California Eagle), the first Black
        newspaper in Los Angeles.

1913   Delta Sigma Theta Sorority was founded at Howard
        University.

        Eva Bowles joined the national staff of the YWCA.

1914   Alice Dunbar-Nelson's Masterpieces of Negro Elo-
        quence was published.

1918   Vada Somerville became the first Black woman grad-
        uated from the School of Dentistry, University of
        Southern California.

        Dr. Ruth Temple was graduated from Loma Linda
        Medical College, becoming its first woman graduate.

1920   Lillian Evanti was hailed as the first Negro to sing
        operatic roles in Europe.

        Zeta Phi Beta Sorority was founded at Howard Uni-
        versity.

1921   Alice Dunbar-Nelson and Robert Nelson founded the
        Wilmington Advocate, a weekly newspaper, in Wil-
        mington, Delaware.

        Vivian Osborn Marsh, founder of Delta Sigma Theta
        in the West, founded the first Western chapter, Kappa,

at the University of California, Berkeley.

1922   The name of Frances Ellen Harper, poet, novelist,
        lecturer, was placed on the Red Letter Calendar at
        the World's Meeting of the Women's Christian Tem-
        perance Union.

1923   Opportunity: Journal of Negro Life was born.

1926   Florence Mills appeared in Blackbirds, a Broadway
        show.

1927   Miriam Matthews, collector of Black art, books,
        documents, photographs, was the first Black profes-
        sional librarian hired by the Los Angeles Public Li-
        brary.

1929   Fay M. Jackson, first American Black woman foreign
        news correspondent, co-founded Flash, a weekly
        news magazine.

        Mirriam Matthews, retired librarian, was the "first
        person to stimulate interest in the celebration of
        Negro History Week" when she sent articles and
        book reviews to local newspapers, city schools, and
        community organizations.

1930   Historian Ida Tarbell named Mary McLeod Bethune
        as one of America's fifty leading women.

1931   Alice Dunbar-Nelson, author, journalist, teacher,
        pioneered with radio station KADN, Wilmington,
        Delaware.

1933   George Gershwin invited Eva Jessye to become the
        choral director of his first Porgy and Bess produc-
        tion.

1937   Fay M. Jackson, former managing editor of the Cali-
        fornia News and co-founder of Flash, a weekly news
        magazine, covered the coronation of King George VI
        and made a special presentation before the French
        Parliament for the Associated Negro Press.

1939   Bernice Bruington became the first Black high school
        principal in Los Angeles.

Miriam Matthews, first Black professional librarian hired by the Los Angeles Public Library

The Daughters of the American Revolution denied
Marian Anderson the right to sing in Constitution
Hall, Washington, D. C.

1940   Katherine Dunham made her dance debut in New
York.

Pearl Primus received a scholarship from the New
Dance Group.

1943   Dr. Ruth Temple organized and founded the Community Health Association, Inc., a health study club,
in Los Angeles.

1943   Katherine Dunham, dancer, was guest artist for the
San Francisco Symphony.

1945   Mademoiselle Magazine selected Gwendolyn Brooks
as one of the ten women of the year.

Dr. Ruth Temple developed the concept of Community Health Week, now proclaimed a permanent insti-
tution in California by the California Legislature.

1947   Hattie McDaniel won the Academy Award for her
role in "Gone With the Wind."

1948   Charlotta Bass, editor of the California Eagle, and
a founding member of the Progressive Party, became the National Co-Chairman of Women for Henry
Wallace.

1950   Zelma George performed in the Broadway production,
The Medium, by Gian Carlo Menotti.

Gwendolyn Brooks won the Pulitzer Prize for her
volume of poems, Annie Allen.

1952   Charlotta Bass became the first Black woman to
run for the second highest office in the land, as Vice
Presidential candidate on the Progressive Party
ticket.

1955   Marian Anderson became another pioneer Black when
she sang the role of Ulrica in Verdi's Masked Ball
at the Metropolitan Opera House.

Rosa Parks, a Black seamstress in Montgomery, Alabama, was arrested on December 1 for refusing to move to the back of the bus. Her arrest led to the Montgomery Bus Boycott.

1956   Ann Arnold Hedgeman, sociologist, educator, civil rights leader, became the first Black woman to run for city-wide office in a major party primary election in New York City.

Authurine Lucy was admitted, then suspended from the University of Alabama.

1957   Daisy Bates directed students in their efforts to integrate schools in Little Rock, Arkansas.

1959   "Raisin in the Sun," written by Lorraine Hansberry, became a Broadway hit and won the Drama Critics' Award.

Marian Anderson was appointed American Lady of Goodwill, Human Rights Committee, U.S. Delegation to the United Nations.

1961   Leontyne Price was given the title role in a Metropolitan opera production.

1962   The California Legislature resolved that Community Health Week, a concept designed by Dr. Ruth Temple, be held the third week in March.

1965   Patricia Roberts Harris was appointed Ambassador to Luxembourg by President Lyndon Johnson.

Aileen C. Hernandez was appointed to the Equal Employment Opportunity Commission (EEOC).

1966   Margaret Walker, educator and poet, published Jubilee, a historical novel, after researching her subject for 34 years. The heroine was Mrs. Walker's great-grandmother.

Constance Baker Motley was appointed a federal judge by President Lyndon B. Johnson.

Yvonne Brathwaite Burke won a seat in the California State Assembly.

1967   Dr. Jean Cooke Wright became Associate Dean of
        New York Medical College.

1968   Gwendolyn Brooks became Poet Laureate of Illinois,
        succeeding Carl Sandburg.

        Diahann Carroll starred in the television show Julia.

        Shirley Chisholm became the first Black woman
        elected to the Congress of the United States.

        Ella Fitzgerald was given the New York City Cul-
        tural Award.

        Elizabeth Koontz was elected President of the Na-
        tional Educational Association.

        Margaret Ann Shaw (Mrs. Leslie N. Shaw) visited
        England, Russia, Hungary and Czechoslovakia as a
        member of a delegation of "outstanding American
        women" at the invitation of the Institute of Soviet-
        American Relations and the Women's Soviet Commit-
        tee in a "woman-to-woman diplomacy program."

        Agnes Wilson was named "Teacher of the Year" by
        the state of South Carolina, becoming the first Black
        to win that award in South Carolina.

1969   Margaret Douroux, composer, choral director, coun-
        selor, teacher, received the best song award from
        the James Cleveland Academy of Gospel Music for
        her composition "Give Me a Clean Heart," and she
        received the A.C.C. Pauline Musician Achievement
        Award.

1972   Yvonne Brathwaite Burke became the first Black
        woman to serve as Vice Chairman of the Democratic
        National Convention; and she was the first Black wo-
        man from California to be elected to Congress.

        Shirley Chisholm, the first Black woman to serve in
        Congress, was also the first Black woman from a
        major political party to announce her candidacy for
        the Presidency of the United States.

        Barbara Jordan was the first Black woman to be
        elected to Congress from a Southern state and from
        Texas.

1973   Yvonne Brathwaite Burke gave birth to a daughter, becoming the first member of Congress to have a child while in office.

1974   The National Council of Negro Women honored its founder, Mary McLeod Bethune, by dedicating a memorial to her. This statue is the only memorial to a woman and the first to a Black person on public land in Washington, D. C.

1975   Shirley Verrett opened the Metropolitan Opera season with her performance in Rossini's The Siege of Corinth.

1976   Ntozake Shange won worldwide acclaim for her choreo-poem, "For Colored Girls Who Have Considered Suicide/When the Rainbow Is Enuf'."

        The Virginia Union University Women Graduates held their first International Congress, which had as its theme: "The V. U. U. Women Graduates: an Untapped Resource."   The meeting, held at the Virginia Union University, was coordinated by Uvelia Bowen.

1977   Patricia Roberts Harris, former Ambassador to Luxembourg and Dean of the Howard University Law School, became the first Black woman to serve in the Cabinet when President Carter appointed her Director of HUD (Housing and Urban Development).

        The city officials of Lafayette, Alabama, proclaimed a special memoriam for Essie Jones Handy, civic worker, mother, and teacher, who had served the community and surrounding areas for 52 years.

1977   Dottie Stallworth, New Jersey entertainer and music teacher, had her song, "Turn Back Your Thermostat," commercially recorded by the Public Services Electric and Gas Company of New Jersey, New York, and Philadelphia.

PART I

COMPREHENSIVE LISTING

Crystal Carr

1. BIBLIOGRAPHIES AND GUIDES TO COLLECTIONS

Arata, Esther Spring and Nicholas John Rotoli. Black American Playwrights, 1800 to the Present: A Bibliography. Metuchen, N.J.: Scarecrow, 1976.

Baker, Augusta. Books about Negro Life for Children. New York: New York Public Library, 1963.

_____. Stories: A List of Stories to Tell and to Read Aloud. 5th ed. New York: New York Public Library, 1960.

"Black Youth: A Bibliography," Freedomways 15 (Third Quarter, 1975), 226-241.

Brigano, Russell Carl. Black Americans in Autobiography: An Annotated Bibliography of Autobiographies and Auto-biographical Books Written Since the Civil War. Durham, No. Carolina: Duke University, 1974.

Bryant, Barbara. Phoenix Films. New York: Phoenix Films, 470 Park Avenue, South. (Bibliography of audio visual films for elementary, junior high and high school.)

Carr, Crystal. Ebony Jewels: A Selected Bibliography of Books by and about Black Women. Rev. ed. Inglewood, Ca.: Crenshaw-Imperial Branch Library, 1975.

Cole, Johnnetta B. "Black Women in America: An Annotated Bibliography," Black Scholar 3:4 (December, 1971), 42-53.

Davis, Lenwood G. The Black Woman in American Society: A Selected Annotated Bibliography. Boston: G. K. Hall, 1975.

Fisher, Edith Maureen. Focusing on Afro-American Research: A Guide on Annotated Bibliography. Ethnic Studies Publication #1. San Diego: University of

California, San Diego, 1975.

George, Zelma. A Guide to Negro Music: An Annotated
    Bibliography of Negro Folk and Art Music by Negro
    Composers or Based on Negro Thematic Material.
    New York University, 1953; Ann Arbor, Michigan: Uni-
    versity Microfilms.

_____. Bibliographical Index to Negro Music. Master
    catalogue of 9,592 titles, in Moreland Collection, How-
    ard University. Washington, D. C. , 1944.

Guide to Manuscripts and Archives in the Negro Collection
    of Trevor Arnett Library, Atlanta University. Atlanta:
    Atlanta University, 1971.

Guzman, Jessie P. "An Annotated List of Books by or Con-
    cerning Negroes in the United States, in Africa and in
    Latin America, 1938-1946," Negro Yearbook, 1947.
    Tuskegee Institute: Department of Records and Re-
    search (DRR).

_____. Civil Rights and the Negro: A List of References
    Relative to Present Day Discussion. Tuskegee Institute,
    Alabama: DRR, 1950.

_____. Desegregation and the Southern States, 1957.
    Legal Action and Voluntary Group Action. With Wood-
    row W. Hall. Tuskegee Institute, Alabama: DRR, 1958.

_____. George Washington Carver, a Classified Bibli-
    ography. Tuskegee Institute, Alabama: DRR, 1953.

_____. George Washington Carver, a Classified Bibliog-
    raphy. Tuskegee Institute, Alabama: DRR, 1955.

_____. "George Washington Carver: A Classified Bibli-
    ography," Bulletin of Bibliography 21:1 (May-August,
    1953), 12-16; Part 2 in 21:2 (September-December,
    1953), 34-39.

Hutson, Jean Blackwell. "African Materials in the Schom-
    burg Collection of Negro Literature and History," Afri-
    can Studies Bulletin 3 (May, 1960), 1-14.

Matthews, Mirriam. "The Negro in California from 1781 to
    1916: An Annotated Bibliography." A Report submitted

to the Graduate School of Library Science, University of Southern California, in partial fulfillment of the requirements for the research course in Library Science 290ab, February 1944.

Maultsby, Portia K. "Selective Bibliography: U.S. Black Music," Ethnomusicology 3:19 (September, 1975), 421-449.

Moseley, Vivian H. "Selected Bibliography on Guidance in Business Education." In Guidance Problems and Procedures in Business Education. Somerville, N.J.: Somerset Press, for the Eastern Business Teachers Association and the National Business Teachers Association, 1954.

Murphy, Beatrice. Bibliographic Survey: The Negro in Print. 117 R Street, N.E. Washington, D.C. 20002 (No longer published).

Perry, Margaret. A Bio-Bibliography of Countee P. Cullen, 1903-1946. Foreword by Don M. Wolfe. Westport, Conn.: Greenwood Publishing Corporation, 1971.

Porter, Dorothy B. "The African Collection at Howard University," African Studies Bulletin 2 (January, 1959), 17-21.

_____. "Library Sources for the Study of Negro Life and History," Journal of Negro Education 5 (April, 1936), 232-244.

_____. The Negro in the United States. Ann Arbor, Mich.: University Microfilms, 1959.

_____. North American Negro Poets: A Bibliographical Check List of Their Writings (1760-1944). Hattiesburg, Miss.: The Book Farm, 1945. Reprinted, New York: Burt Franklin, 1963.

_____. A Working Bibliography on the Negro in the United States. Ann Arbor, Mich.: University Microfilms, 1969.

_____, and Ethel M. Ellis. Index to the Journal of Negro Education, Vols. 1-31. Washington, D.C.: Howard University, 1953.

Ramsly, Arnette M., ed. Directory: National Black Peri-
odicals and Journals. Harlem: Afram Assn., Inc.,
1972.

Rollins, Charlemae Hill. We Build Together: A Reader's
Guide to Negro Life and Literature for Elementary and
High School. Chicago: National Council of Teachers of
English, 1967.

Smith, Jessie Carney. "Developing Collections of Black Literature," Black World 20 (June, 1971), 18-29.

_____. "The Research Collections in Negro Life and Cul-
ture at Fisk University." A paper presented before the
workshop on Bibliographic Resources for a Study of the
American Negro. Washington, D.C.: Howard University Library, July 22-26, 1968.

_____. "Research Resources in Negro Life and Culture."
A paper presented at and published in the proceedings
of a summer workshop on Social Sciences Approaches
to the Study of the Negro, held at Fisk University,
1968.

Southern, Eileen. "William Grant Still: List of Major
Works," Black Perspectives in Music 2:3 (May, 1971),
235-238.

Tolson, Ruth M. Hampton Institute Press Publications, a
Bibliography. Hampton, Virginia: Hampton Institute,
1958.

Williams, Ora. "A Bibliography of Works Written by American Black Women," CLA Journal 15:3 (March, 1972),
354-377.

_____. "Works by and about Alice Ruth (Moore) Dunbar-
Nelson: A Bibliography," CLA Journal 3:19 (March,
1976), 322-326.

Young, Carlene. "Black Scholar and the Social Sciences,"
Black Scholar 7:7 (April, 1976), 18-28.

Young, Pauline A. "The American Negro: A Bibliography
for School Libraries," Wilson Library Bulletin 7 (May,
1953), 563.

2. ENCYCLOPEDIAS, HANDBOOKS, AND OTHER REFERENCE BOOKS

Cedarholm, Theresa. Afro-American Artists: A Bio-Bibliographical Directory. Boston: Boston Public Library, 1973.

Clark, Chris and Sheila Rush. How to Get Along with Black People: A Handbook. Foreword by Bill Cosby. New York: Joseph A. Opaku, Inc., 1971.

Dannett, Sylvia G. L. Profiles of Negro Womanhood. Vol. I, 1619-1900; Vol. II, 20th Century. Yonkers, N.Y.: Educational Heritage, 1964. (Negro Heritage Library)

Davis, John P., ed. American Negro Reference Book. Englewood Cliffs, N.J.: Prentice-Hall, 1966.

Dillard, Clarissa and Uvelia Bowen, eds. Virginia Union University Women Graduates: Resource Registry, 1976. Richmond: International Congress of Virginia Union University Graduates, 1976.

Guzman, Jessie Parkhurst. The Negro Yearbook. A Review of Events Affecting Negro Life, 1941-1946. Tuskegee Institute, Alabama: DRR, 1947.

_____. The Negro Year Book. A Review of Events Affecting Negro Life, 1947-1951. New York: William H. Wise and Co., Inc., 1952.

Levi, Doris J. and Nerissa L. Milton. Directory of Black Literary Magazines. Washington: Negro Bibliographic and Research Center, Inc., 1972.

Murray, Florence. Negro Handbook. New York: Malliet, 1942.

7

The Negro Handbook. Comp. by Editors of Ebony. Chicago:
    Johnson Publ. Co., 1966.

The Negro Handbook: An Annual Encyclopedia of the Negro.
    Tuskegee Institute, Alabama: DRR, 1912-1967.

Pack, Leaoneda Bailey, comp. and ed. Broadside Authors
    and Artists: An Illustrated Biographical Dictionary.
    Detroit, Mich.: Broadside Press, 1974.

Romero, P. J. In Black America, 1968: The Year of
    Awakening. Washington, D.C.: United Publishing
    Corporation, 1969.

Wells, Ida B. A Red Record: Lynchings in the United
    States, 1892-1893-1894. Chicago, 1894. Reprinted,
    New York: Arno Press, 1971.

3. AUTOBIOGRAPHIES AND BIOGRAPHIES
BY BLACK WOMEN

Adams, Elizabeth Laura. Dark Symphony. New York: Sheed
and Ward, 1942.

Alexander, Sadie T. M. Who's Who Among Negro Lawyers.
Biographical sketches of 219 of 1200 American Negro
Lawyers, and names and addresses of 136 others. Phil-
adelphia: National Bar Association, n. d.

Anderson, Marian. My Lord, What a Morning. New York:
Viking, 1956.

Angelou, Maya. Gather Together in My Name. New York:
Random House, 1974.

_____. I Know Why the Caged Bird Sings. New York:
Random House, 1969.

Bailey, Pearl. The Raw Pearl. New York: Pocket Books,
1969.

_____. Talking to Myself. New York: Harcourt, 1973
(paperback).

Barlow, Leila Mae. Across the Years: Memoirs. Montgomery, Alabama: The Paragon Press, 1959.

Bass, Charlotta A. Forty Years: Memoirs from the Pages
of a Newspaper. Los Angeles: Charlotta A. Bass,
1960.

Bates, Daisy. The Long Shadow of Little Rock. New York:
David McKay Co. , 1962.

Beasley, Delilah L. The Negro Trail Blazers of California.
A Compilation of Records from the California Archives

9

at Bancróft Library, University of California at Berkeley;
also from diaries, old papers, conversations of old pioneers in California. Los Angeles, 1919.

Bethune, Mary McLeod. "My Last Will and Testament,"
Ebony 29:5 (March, 1974), 44-50.

Bilbrew, A. C. "Report on the Status of the American Negro
Women of Yesterday, Today, and Tomorrow." For a
women's meeting held in Copenhagen, Denmark, April
21-24, 1960. Los Angeles: The Sojourner Truth Industrial Club, Inc., n.d.

Boone-Jones, Margaret. Martin Luther King, Jr.: A Pic-
ture Story. Illus. by R. Scott. Chicago: Children's
Press, 1968.

_____. To Be Somebody: Portrait of Nineteen Beautiful
Detroiters. New York: Vantage Press, 1976.

Brown, Hallie Q. "Victoria Earle Matthews." In Homespun
Heroines. Zenia, Ohio: Aldine, 1926.

_____, ed. Homespun Heroines and Other Women of Dis-
tinction. Foreword by Mrs. Josephine Turpin. Xenia,
Ohio: Aldine, 1926.

Brown, Josephine. Biography of an American Bondsman, by
His Daughter. Boston: R. F. Wallcut, 1855.

Browne, Rose Butler. Love My Children. New York: Mere-
dith Press, 1969.

Browning, Alice C. Lionel Hampton's Swing Book. Chicago:
Negro Story Press, 1949.

Burke, Yvonne Brathwaite. "The Kind of World I Want for
My Child," Ebony 29:5 (March, 1974), 149-153.

Cherry, Gwendolyn, and others. Portraits in Color: The
Times of Colorful Negro Women. New York: Pageant
Press, 1962.

Chesnutt, Helen. Charles Waddell Chesnutt: Pioneer of the
Color Line. Chapel Hill: University of North Carolina
Press, 1952.

Childress, Alice. "Tribute," Freedomways 11 (First Quarter, 1971), 14-15 (Paul Robeson).

Chisholm, Shirley. Unbought and Unbossed. New York: Avon Publishers, 1952.

Clark, Septima (Poinsette) with LeGette Blythe. Echo in My Soul. Foreword by Harry Golden. New York: Dutton, 1962.

Clifton, Lucille. Generations: A Memoir. New York: Random House, 1976.

Cole, Maria Ellington and Louie Robinson. Nat King Cole: An Intimate Biography. New York: Morrow, 1972.

Cooper, Anna Julia (Haywood). A Voice from the South, by a Black Woman of the South. Xenia, Ohio: Aldine, 1892.

Coppin, Fannie Jackson. Reminiscenses of School Life, Hints on Teaching. Philadelphia: AME Book Concern, 1913.

Daniels, Sadie Iola. Women Builders. Rev. and ed. by Charles H. Wesley and Thelma D. Perry. Washington, D. C. : Arno Press, 1970.

Davis, Angela. Angela Davis: An Autobiography. New York: Random House, 1974.

Dawson, Osceola Aleese. The Timberlake Store. Carbondale, Ill. : Dunaway-Sinclair, 1959.

Dillard, Clarissa and Uvelia Bowen, eds. Virginia Union University Women Graduates: Resource Registry, 1976. Richmond: International Congress of Virginia Union University Graduates, 1976.

DuBois, Shirley Graham. "Tribute to Paul Robeson," Freedomways (First Quarter, 1971), 6-7.

_____. Your Most Humble Servant: The Story of Benjamin Banneker. New York: Messner, 1949.

Dunbar-Nelson, Alice Ruth Moore. "The Life of Social Service as Exemplified in David Livingstone." In

Masterpieces of Negro Eloquence. New York: The Book-
ery Publishing Co. , 1914; Johnson Reprint Corp. , 1970.
(Speech delivered at Lincoln University, Pennsylvania,
March 7, 1913).

Dunham, Katherine. Touch of Innocence. New York and
London: Cassell, 1960.

Edmonds, Helen G. Black Faces in High Places. New York:
Harcourt, 1971.

Ferris, Luanne. I'm Done Crying, as told to Beth Day.
New York: New American Library, 1970.

Forten, Charlotte L. The Journal of Charlotte L. Forten,
ed. by Ray Allen Billington. New York: Collier Books,
1961.

_____. "Life on Sea Islands." In The Negro Caravan, ed.
by Sterling A. Brown and others. New Introduction by
Julius Lester. New York: Arno Press, 1970.

Gibson, Althea. I Always Wanted to Be Somebody. New
York: Harper, 1958.

Giovanni, Nikki. Gemini: An Extended Autobiographical
Statement on My Twenty-Five Years of Being a Black
Poet. Indianapolis: Bobbs-Merrill, 1971.

_____, and Margaret Walker. A Poetic Equation: Conver-
sations Between Nikki Giovanni and Margaret Walker.
Washington, D.C. : Howard University Press, 1974.

Graham, Shirley. Booker T. Washington. New York: Messner, 1955.

_____. George Washington Carver. New York: Messner,
1944.

_____. John Baptiste DeSable. New York: Messner,
1953.

_____. Julius K. Nyerere: Teacher of Africa. New York:
Messner, 1975.

_____. The Story of Paul Robeson. New York: Messner,
1967.

_____. The Story of Phillis Wheatley. New York: Mess-
ner, 1949.

_____. There Once Was a Slave: The Heroic Story of
Frederick Douglas. New York: Messner, 1947.

Greenfield, Eloise. Paul Robeson. New York: Crowell,
1975.

_____. Rosa Parks. New York: Crowell, 1973.

Gresham, Jewell Handy, ed. "James Baldwin Comes Home,"
Essence 7 (June, 1976), 54, 55, 80, 82, 85, 86.

Griffin, Judith Berry. Nat Turner. Illus. by Leo Carty.
New York: Coward, McCann and Geoghegan, 1970.

Griffiths, Mattie. Autobiography of a Female Slave. New
York: New York Universities Press, 1857.

Grimke, Angelina W. A Biographical Sketch of Archibald H.
Grimke. New York: Arno Press, 1970.

Guffy, Ossie. Ossie: The Autobiography of a Black Woman,
as told to Caryl Ledner. New York: W. W. Norton
and Co., Inc., 1971.

Guzman, Jessie Parkhurst. "Monroe Nathan Work and His
Contributions," Journal of Negro History 34:5 (October,
1949), 428-461.

_____. "W. E. B. DuBois--The Historian," Journal of
Negro History 30:4 (Fall, 1961), 377-385.

Hamilton, Virginia. Paul Robeson: The Life and Times of
a Free Black Man. New York: Harper, 1974.

Hansberry, Lorraine. "The Legacy of W. E. B. DuBois."
In Black Titan: W. E. B. DuBois, ed. by John Henrik
Clarke and others. Boston: Beacon Press, 1970.

_____. "My Name Is Lorraine Hansberry, I Am a Writer,"
Esquire, November, 1969, 140.

_____. To Be Young, Gifted and Black: Lorraine Hans-
berry in Her Words. Adapted by Robert Nemiroff.
Englewood Cliffs, N. J.: Prentice-Hall, 1969. (Also

includes selections of her work.)

Hare, Maud Cuney. Norris Wright Cuney: A Tribute to
Black People. Introduction by Robert C. Cotner. New
York: The Crisis Publishing Co., 1913; Austin, Texas:
Steck-Vaughn, 1968.

Hedgeman, Anna (Arnold). The Trumpet Sounds. New York:
Holt Rinehart & Winston, 1964.

Hicks, Nora Louise. Slave Girl Reba and Her Descendants
in America. New York: Exposition Press, 1974.

Holiday, Billie. Lady Sings the Blues. New York: Doubleday, 1956.

Holley, Miller Allie. "Alice Ruth Moore Dunbar-Nelson:
The Individual." Biographical sketch written for Delta
Sigma Theta Regional Conference, Sheraton Charles
Hotel, June 2-5, 1968.

Horne, Lena. Lena. New York: Doubleday, 1965.

Hunter, Jane Edna. A Nickel and a Prayer. Nashville,
Tenn.: The Parthenon Press, 1940.

Hurston, Zora N. Dust Tracks on a Road. Philadelphia:
Lippincott, 1942.

Jackson, Harrisene. There's Nothing I Own That I Want.
Englewood Cliffs, N.J.: Prentice-Hall, 1974.

Jackson, Mahalia. Movin' Up. New York: Avon, 1969.

Jones, Hettie. Big Star Fallin Mama: Five Women in Black
Music. New York: Viking, 1974.

Keckley, Elizabeth. "The Death of Lincoln." In The Negro
Caravan, ed. by Sterling Brown et al. New York: Arno Press, 1970.

King, Coretta Scott. My Life with Martin Luther King, Jr.
New York: Holt Rinehart & Winston, 1969.

Kitt, Eartha. Thursday's Child. New York: Duell, Sloan
and Pearce, 1956.

Majors, Gerri, with Doris Saunders. Black Society. Chicago: Johnson Publishing Company, 1977.

Masso, Clara Bodian. "On Mary McLeod Bethune and the National Council of Negro Women," Freedomways 1 (Fourth Quarter, 1974), 51-53.

Matthews, Mirriam. "Alice Taylor Gafford," Family Savings Community News Letter 1:1 (October, 1967), 1, 3.

_____. "Beaulah Ecton Woodard." Part of Beulah Woodard Scrapbook sent to Surmondt Museum in Aachen, Germany, 1954.

_____. "Phylon Profile, XXIII: William Grant Still--Composer," Phylon 12:2 (Second Quarter 1951), 106-112.

Meriwether, Louise. Daddy was a Number Runner. New York: Pyramid Books, 1970/1971.

Montgomery, E[vangeline] J. "Statement: Sargent Claude Johnson." In Black Reflections, I: The Paintings and Sculpture of Sargent Johnson/Charles Dawkins. San Francisco: Sanderson Museum of the San Francisco African-American Historical and Cultural Society, Inc., 1976.

Moody, Anne. Coming of Age in Mississippi. New York: Dell, 1968.

Mossell, Mrs. Gertrude E. The Work of the Afro-American Woman. Philadelphia: C. S. Ferguson Co., 1908 (© 1894).

Murray, Pauli. Proud Shoes: The Story of an American Family. New York: Harper and Brothers, 1956.

Petry, Ann. Harriet Tubman. New York: Crowell, 1955.

_____. Tituba of Salem. New York: Crowell, 1964.

Pittman, Evelyn LaRue. Rich Heritage. Oklahoma City: Harlow Publishing Corporation, 1944.

Pitts, Gertrude. Tragedies of Life. Newark, N.J.: The Author, 1939.

Evangeline J. Montgomery.   Photo by Edward Brooks

Porter, Dorothy.   "David Ruggles, 1810-1849: Hydropathic
    Practitioner," Journal of the National Medical Associa-
    tion, 49 (January, 1957), 67-72; and (March, 1957),
    130-134.

Robeson, Eslanda Goode.   "Paul Robeson and the Province-
    towners."   In The Negro Caravan, ed. by Sterling Brown
    et al. New York: Arno Press, 1970.

_____.   Paul Robeson, Negro.   New York: Harper, 1930.

Robinson, Wilhemena S.   "Biographies in Black America,
    1968."   In Black America, ed. by Pat Romero.   Wash-
    ington D. C. : Associated Publishers, 1969.

Rollins, Charlemae Hill.   Black Troubadour: Langston Hughes.
    New York: Rand McNally, 1949.

_____. Famous American Negro Poets. New York: Dodd, Mead, 1965.

_____. Famous Negro Entertainers of Stage, Screen, and TV. New York: Dodd, Mead, 1967.

_____. They Showed the Way: Forty American Negro Leaders. New York: Crowell, 1964.

Schuyler, Philippa Duke. Adventure in Black and White. New York: R. Speller, 1960.

_____. "Meet the George Schuyler's," Our World 6 (April, 1951), 22-26.

_____. "Why I Don't Marry," Ebony 13:9 (July, 1958), 78-80.

Shabazz, Betty. "The Legacy of My Husband, Malcolm X," Ebony 24:8 (June, 1969), 172+.

Sheppard, Gladys. Mary Church Terrell, Respectable Person. Baltimore: Human Relations Press, 1951.

Shockley, Ann. "Pauline Hopkins: A Biographical Excursion into Obscurity," Phylon 33 (Spring, 1972), 22-26.

_____, and Sue P. Chandler. Living Black American Authors: A Biographical Directory. Foreword by Jessie Carney Smith. New York: R. R. Bowker Co., 1973.

Smith, Amanda. An Autobiography of Mrs. Amanda Smith. Chicago: Meyer and Brothers, 1893.

Smith, Jean. "I Learned to Feel Black." In The Black Power Revolt, ed. by Floyd Barbour. Boston: Porter Sargent, 1968.

Southern, Eileen. "Conversations with Fele Sowande, High Priest of Music," Black Perspectives in Music 1:4 (Spring, 1976), 90-107.

Speare, Mrs. Chloe. Memoir of Mrs. Chloe Speare, a Native of Africa Who Was Enslaved in Childhood and Died in Boston Jan. 3, 1815. By a lady of Boston. Boston: J. Louny, 1832.

Tarry, Ellen. Katherine Drexel, Friend of the Neglected.
Illus. by Donald Bolognese. New York: Farrar, Straus
and Cudahy, 1950.

_____. The Third Door: The Autobiography of an Ameri-
can Negro Woman. New York: McKay, 1955.

Taylor, Susie King. Reminiscences of My Life in Camp with
33rd United States Colored Troops. Boston: The Author, 1902.

Terrell, Mary Church. A Colored Woman in a White World.
Washington, D. C. : Ransdell Inc. , 1940.

Thompson, Era Bell. American Daughter. Chicago: Univ.
of Chicago Press, 1946.

_____. "Love Comes to Mahalia," Ebony 20:1 (November,
1964), 50-61.

_____. "The Vaughan Family: A Tale of Two Continents,"
Ebony 30:4 (February, 1975), 53-58.

Thurman, Sue Bailey. Pioneers of Negro Origin in California. San Francisco: Acme Publishing Co. , 1949.

Truth, Sojourner. Sojourner Truth: Narrative and Book of
Life. Chicago: Johnson Publ. Co. , 1970. (Biographies,
essays, and brief commentary on Sojourner Truth.)

Turner, Lucy Mae. "The Family of Nat Turner, 1831-1954,"
Negro History Bulletin 18:6 (March, 1955), 129,132,
145; also 18:7 (April, 1955), 155-158.

Veney, Bethany. The Narrative of Bethany Veny, A Slave
Woman. Introduction by Reverend Bishop Mallalieu, and
commendatory notices from Reverend V. A. Cooper and
Erastus Spaulding. Worcester, Mass. , 1889.

Vivan, Octavia B. Coretta: The Story of Mrs. Martin Luther King, Jr. New York: Fortress Press, 1970.

Vroman, Mary Elizabeth. Shaped to Its Purpose: Delta Sigma Theta, The First Fifty Years. New York: Random
House, 1965.

Waters, Ethel. His Eye Is on the Sparrow. With Charles

Samuels.   Garden City, N. Y. :   Doubleday, 1951.

_____. To Me It's Wonderful. New York: Harper, 1972.

Wells, Ida B.   Crusade for Justice: Autobiography of Ida B.
Wells.   Ed. by Alfreda Duster.   Chicago: Univ. of
Chicago Press, 1970.

Wheatley, Phillis.   Letters of Phillis Wheatley, The Negro
Slave Poet of Boston.   Boston: 1864.

_____. Memoir and Poems of Phillis Wheatley, A Slave.
Boston: Isaac Knapp, 1838.

Williams, Rose Berthena Clay.   Black and White Orange.
New York: Vantage Press, 1961.

Williams, Ruby Ora.   "An In-Depth Portrait of Alice Dunbar-
Nelson. "   Dissertation.   Microfilm or Xerographic
copies, Ann Arbor, Mich. :   University Microfilms, 1974.

Wilson, Beth.   Martin Luther King, Jr.   New York: Putnam,
1973.

Young, Pauline.   "Paul Laurence Dunbar: An Intimate
Glance, "   Freedomways 12 (Fourth Quarter, 1972),
319-329.

4. BIOGRAPHY AND CRITICISM BY AUTHORS OTHER THAN BLACK WOMEN*

Albertson, Chris. Bessie Smith: Empress of the Blues. New York: Schirmer Books, 1975.

Bradford, Sarah Elizabeth (Hopkins). Scenes in the Life of Harriet Tubman. Auburn, N. Y. : W. J. Moses, printer, 1869.

Brownmiller, Susan. Shirley Chisholm: A Biography. New York: Doubleday, 1971.

Burt, Olive W. Mary McLeod Bethune: Girl Devoted to Her People. Illus. by James Cummins. New York: Bobbs-Merrill, 1970.

Butterfield, Stephen. Black Autobiography in America. Amherst: University of Massachusetts, 1974.

Carruth, Ella Kaiser. She Wanted to Read: The Story of Mary McLeod Bethune. Illus. by Herbert McClure. Nashville: Abingdon Press, 1966; New York: Archway Paperback, 1969.

Carson, Josephine. Silent Voices: The Southern Negro Woman Today. New York: Dell, 1971.

Conrad, Earl. Harriet Tubman: Negro Soldier and Abolitionist. New York: International Publishers, 1942.

Cunningham, Virginia. Paul Laurence Dunbar and His Song. New York: Biblo and Tannen, 1969.

Dannett, Sylvia. Profiles of Negro Womanhood, 1619-1900. Vol. I. Yonkers, N. Y. : Educational Heritage, 1964.

* Or not determined to be Black women.

20

Davis, Angela, and other political prisoners. If They Come in the Morning. Foreword by Julian Bond. New York: Joseph A. Opaku, Inc., 1971.

Dodds, Barbara. Negro Literature for High School Students. Urbana, Ill.: National Council of Teachers of English, 1968.

Douty, Esther M. Charlotte Forten: Free Black Teacher. Champaign, Ill.: Garrard Publishing Co., 1971.

DuBois, W. E. B. "The Freedom of Womanhood." In The Gift of Black Folk: The Negroes in the Making of America. New York: Washington Square Press, 1970.

Fiofiori, Tam. "Angela Davis: Portrait of a Revolutionary," Black World 6:21 (April, 1972), 82-84. (Review of a film.)

Ford, Nick Aaron. "Alice Dunbar-Nelson." In Notable American Women, 1607-1950, ed. by Edward T. James et al. Cambridge, Mass.: Harvard-Belknap University Press, 1971.

Goode, Kenneth G. California's Black Pioneers: A Brief Historical Survey. Foreword by Wilson Riles. Santa Barbara, Calif.: McNally and Loftin, 1973.

Harnan, Terry. African Rhythm-American Dance: A Biography of Katherine Dunham. New York: Knopf, 1974.

Hatch, James V., ed. Black Theater, U.S.A.: Forty-Five Plays by Black Americans, 1847-1974. New York: The Free Press, 1974.

Havens, Raymond Dexter. The Influence of Milton on English Poets. New York: Russell and Russell, 1961.

Heidish, Marcy. A Woman Called Moses. Boston: Houghton Mifflin, 1976.

Hemenway, Robert. "Folklore Field Notes from Zora Neale Hurston," Black Scholar 7:7 (April, 1976), 39-46.

Holdredge, Helen. Mammy Pleasant. New York: Ballantine Books, 1972.

Holt, Rockham. Mary McLeod Bethune. New York: Doubleday, 1964.

Jaffe, Dan. "Gwendolyn Brooks: An Appreciation from White
Suburbs." In The Black American Writer, ed. by C.
N. E. Bigsby. Vol. 2. Baltimore: Penguin Books,
1971.

Johnson, Charles S. "Some Books of 1924," Opportunity 26:3
(February, 1925), 59. (Review J. Fauset.)

Katz, Bernard and Jonathan Katz. Black Woman: A Fiction-
alized Biography of Lucy Terry Prince. New York:
Pantheon Books, 1973.

Kent, George E. "The Poetry of Gwendolyn Brooks," Part I,
Black World 11:20 (September, 1971), 30-43.

_____. "The Poetry of Gwendolyn Brooks," Part II, Black
World 12:20 (October, 1971), 36-48, 68-71.

Larison, Cornelius Wilson. Silvia DuBois (Now 116 Years
Old): A Biography of the Slav Who Whipt and Gand Her
Freedom. Ringer, N.J., 1883.

Lewis, Alice A. "Angela Davis in Port Gibson, Mississippi,"
Freedomways 2:15 (Second Quarter, 1975), 114-117.

McFarlin, Annjennette Sophie. Black Congressional Reconstruction Orators and Their Orations, 1869-1879. Metuchen, N.J.: Scarecrow, 1976.

McMillan, Lewick. "Mary Lou Williams: First Lady of
Jazz," Downbeat 38 (May 27, 1971), 16-17.

McPherson, James M. and others. Blacks in America:
Bibliographical Essays. New York: Anchor Books,
1972.

Martin, Jay, ed. A Singer in the Dawn: A Reinterpretation
of Paul Laurence Dunbar. New York: Dodd, Mead,
1975.

Mather, Frank Lincoln. Who's Who of the Colored Race: A
General Biographical Dictionary of Men and Women of
African Descent. Detroit: Gale Research Co., 1975;
reprint of edition published in Chicago, 1915.

Miller, Adam David. "Brown Girl, Brownstones," Black
      Scholar 9:3 (May, 1972), 56-58.

The Negro Handbook. Compiled by editors of Ebony. Chica-
      go: Johnson Publ. Co., 1966.

Ortiz, Victoria. Sojourner Truth: A Self-Made Woman.
      Philadelphia: Lippincott, 1974.

Parker, J. A. Angela Davis: The Making of a Revolution-
      ary. New York: Arlington House, 1973.

Parks, Carole A. "J. E. Franklin, Playwright," Black
      World 6:21 (April, 1972), 49-50.

Peare, Catherine O. Mary McLeod Bethune. New York:
      Vanguard Press, 1951.

Peterson, Helen Stone. Sojourner Truth: Fearless Crusader.
      Illus. by Victory Mays. Champaign, Ill.: Garrard
      Publishing Co., 1972.

"Phillis Wheatley." In Early Negro American Writers, ed.
      by Benjamin Brawley. New York: Dover Publications,
      Inc., 1970.

Professor, The. Angela: A Revealing Close-Up of the Wo-
      man. North Hollywood, Calif.: Leisure Books, 1971.

Richmond, M. A. Bid the Vassal Soar: Interpretative Es-
      says on the Life and Poetry of Phillis Wheatley and
      George Moses Horton. Washington, D. C.: Howard
      Univ. Press, 1974.

Schuyler, Josephine. Philippa, the Beautiful American: The
      Traveled History of a Troubadour. New York: Philip-
      pa Schuyler Memorial Fund, 1969.

Sherman, Joan R. Invisible Poets: Afro-Americans of the
      Nineteenth Century. Urbana, Ill.: University of Illinois
      Press, 1974.

Staples, Robert. The Black Woman in America. Chicago:
      Nelson-Hall, 1973.

Sterling, Philip and Rayford Logan. Four Took Freedom:
      The Lives of Harriet Tubman, Frederick Douglass,

Robert Smalls, and Blanche K. Bruce. New York:
Doubleday, 1967.

Titus, Frances W. Narrative of Sojourner Truth: A Bonds-
woman of Olden Time. New York: Arno Press, 1970.

"Votes for Women: A Symposium by Leading Thinkers of
Colored America," Crisis 4:10 (August, 1915), 178-192.

Winders, Gertrude Hecker. Harriet Tubman: Freedom Girl.
Illus. by William K. Plummer. New York: Bobbs-
Merrill, 1969.

"Woman Suffrage," Crisis 1:11 (November, 1915), 29-30.

"Women's Rites." Review of For Colored Girls Who Have
Considered Suicide/When the Rainbow is Enuf', by
Ntozake Shange. Newsweek, June 14, 1976, p. 99.

5. ANTHOLOGIES AND COLLECTIONS

a) Black Women Editors

Alexander, Rae P., ed. Young and Black in America. New York: Random House, 1972.

[Bambara], Toni Cade, ed. Tales and Stories for Black Folks. New York: Doubleday, 1971.

Booker, Sue. Cry at Birth. New York: McGraw-Hill, 1971.

Brooks, Gwendolyn, ed. Jump Bad: A New Chicago Anthology. Detroit: Broadside Press, 1971. (Fiction, poetry, reviews, criticism.)

Brown, Patricia L. and others. To Gwen with Love. Chicago: Johnson Publ. Co., 1971.

Childress, Alice, ed. Black Scenes. New York: Doubleday, 1971.

Collier, Eugenia W. and Richard A. Long, eds. Afro-American Writing. 2 vols. New York: New York University Press, 1972.

Davis, Angela Y. and other political prisoners. If They Come in the Morning. Foreword by Julian Bond. New York: Joseph A. Opaku, Inc., 1971.

Dee, Ruby, ed. Glowchild and Other Poems. New York: Third Press, 1972.

Detroit Public Schools. Afro-America Sings. Prepared by a Detroit Public Schools Workshop under the direction of Ollie McFarland. Editorial direction, John W. Pritchard. Detroit: The Board of Education of the School District of Detroit, 1971.

Dunbar-Nelson, Alice Ruth (Moore), ed. The Dunbar Speaker
and Entertainer. Naperville, Ill. : J. L. Nichols &
Co. , 1920.

_____. Masterpieces of Negro Eloquence. New York:
The Bookery Publishing Co. , 1914; Johnson Reprint Co. ,
1970.

Exum, Pat Crutchfield. Keeping the Faith: Writings by Contemporary Black American Women. Greenwich, Conn. :
Fawcett Publications, Inc. , 1974.

Giovanni, Nikki, ed. Night Comes Softly: Anthology of Black
Female Voices. New York: Nik-Tom Publications,
1970.

Guy, Rosa. Children of Longing. New York: Bantam, 1970.
(Essays written by young Blacks in rural and urban
U. S. A.)

Jordan, June, ed. Soulscript: Afro-American Poetry. New
York: Zenith, 1970.

Kelly, Ernece, ed. Points of Departure. New York: John
Wiley, 1972.

Lane, Pinkie Gordon, ed. Discourses in Poetry. 6th Annual
Ed. Fort Smith, Ark. : South and West Publishers,
1972.

Littleton, Arthur and Mary W. Burger, eds. Black Viewpoints. New York: New American Library, 1971.
(Essays.)

Love, Rose L. , ed. A Collection of Folklore for Children in
Elementary School and at Home. New York: Vantage
Press, 1964.

Maultsby, Portia K. with Gerard Behague. Ethnomusicology
3:19 (September, 1974).

Miller, Ruth, ed. Backgrounds to Blackamerican Literature.
Scranton, Pa. : Chandler Publishing Co. , 1970.

_____. Blackamerican Literature: 1970-Present. Fore-
ward by John Hope Franklin. Beverly Hills, Calif. :
Glencoe Press, 1971.

Montgomery, E[vangeline] J. California Black Craftsmen. Catalogue of Exhibit held February 15, 1970-March 8, 1970. Oakland: Mills College Art Gallery, 1970.

Murphy, Beatrice, ed. Ebony Rhythm. New York: Exposition, 1948.

_____. Negro Voices: An Anthology of Contemporary Verse. New York: Harrison, 1938.

_____. Today's Negro Voices: An Anthology by Young Negro Poets. New York: Messner, 1970.

Murray, Alma and Robert Thomas. Black Perspectives. New York: Scholastic Book Services, 1971.

Porter, Dorothy, ed. Early Negro Writing, 1760-1840. Boston: Beacon Press, 1970. (Collection of Black history, literature, music at Howard University, Washington, D.C.)

Randall, Dudley and Margaret G. Burroughs, eds. For Malcolm: Poems on the Life and the Death of Malcolm X. Preface and eulogy by Ossie Davis. Detroit: Broadside Press, 1967.

_____, and Margaret Danner. Poem Counterpoem. Detroit: Broadside Press, 1966.

Rollins, Charlemae Hill. Christmas Gift: An Anthology of Christmas Poems, Songs and Stories Written by and about Negroes. Chicago: Follett, 1963.

Sanchez, Sonia. We Be Word Sorcerers: 25 Stories by Black Americans. New York: Bantam, 1973.

Spradling, Mary Mace, ed. In Black and White: Afro-American in Print. Kalamazoo, Mich.: Kalamazoo Library System, 1971.

Washington, Mary Helen, ed. Black-Eyed Susans: Classic Stories by and about Black Women. New York: Anchor Books, 1975.

Williams, Jayme Coleman and McDonald Williams, eds. The Negro Speaks: The Rhetoric of Contemporary Black Leaders. New York: Noble and Noble, 1971.

Williams, Paulette, ed. Phat Mama. Vol. 1. New York:
    P. M. Inc., 1970.

b) Non-Black Women Editors

Adoff, Arnold, ed. Brothers and Sisters. New York: Dell,
    1970.

_____. The Poetry of Black America: Anthology of the
    20th Century. Introduction by Gwendolyn Brooks. New
    York: Harper, 1973.

Alhamsi, Ahmed and Harun Kofi Wangara, eds. Black Arts:
    An Anthology of Black Creations. Detroit: Black Arts
    Publications, 1969.

Barbour, Floyd B., ed. The Black Power Revolt. Boston:
    Porter Sargent, 1968.

Barksdale, Richard and Kenneth Kinnamon. Black Writers of
    America. New York: Macmillan, 1972.

Bontemps, Arna, ed. American Negro Poetry. New York:
    Hill and Wang, 1963.

_____, and Langston Hughes, eds. The Poetry of the Ne-
    gro, 1746-1949. New York: Doubleday, 1953.

Botkin, B. A., ed. Lay My Burden Down: A Folk History
    of Slavery. Chicago: Univ. of Chicago Press, 1945.

Boulware, Marcus Manna, ed. The Oratory of Negro Lead-
    ers: 1900-1968. Westport, Conn.: Negro Universities
    Press, 1969.

Brasner, William and Dominick Consolo, eds. Black Drama:
    An Anthology. Introduction by Darwin T. Turner. Co-
    lumbus, Ohio: Charles Merrill, 1970.

Brawley, Benjamin, ed. Early Negro American Writers.
    New York: Dover Publications, Inc., 1970.

Brown, Sterling and others, eds. The Negro Caravan. Intro-
    duction by Julius Lester. New York: Arno Press, 1970.

Bullins, Ed, ed. New Plays from the Black Theatre. To-
ronto: Bantam, 1969.

Chapman, Abraham, ed. Black Voices. New York: New
American Library, 1968.

Clarke, John Henrik, ed. Harlem, U.S.A. Berlin: Seven
Seas Publishers, 1964.

Coombs, Orde, ed. What We Must See: Young Black Story-
tellers. New York: Dodd, Mead, 1971.

Couch, William Jr., ed. New Black Playwrights. Baton
Rouge, La.: Louisiana State University Press, 1968.

Davis, Charles and Daniel Walden. On Being Black. Greenwich: Fawcett Publications, Inc., 1970.

Emanuel, James A. and Theodore Gross, eds. Dark Symphony: Negro Literature in America. New York: The
Free Press, 1968.

Ford, Nick Aaron. Black Insights. Waltham, Mass.: Ginn
and Co., 1971.

_____, and H. L. Faggett, eds. Best Short Stories by
Afro-American Writers, 1925-1950. Boston: Meador,
1950.

Gayle, Addison, ed. Black Expression: Essays by and about
Black Americans in the Creative Arts. New York:
Weybright and Talley, 1969.

Hayden, Robert and others, eds. Afro-American Literature:
An Introduction. New York: Harcourt, 1971.

Hill, Herbert, ed. Soon, One Morning: New Writing by
American Negroes, 1940-1962. New York: Knopf, 1968.

Hughes, Langston, ed. The Best Short Stories by Negro
Writers: An Anthology from 1899 to the Present. Boston: Little, Brown, 1967.

Jones, LeRoi and Larry Neal, eds. Black Fire: An Anthology of Afro-American Writing. New York: Morrow,
1968.

Kerlin, Robert, ed. Negro Poets and Their Poems. 3rd ed.
Washington, D. C: Associated Publishers, 1923.

King, Woodie, ed. Black Spirits: A Festival of New Black
Poets in America. Foreword by Nikki Giovanni. New
York: Vintage, 1972.

Lee, Don L., ed. Dynamite Voices: Black Poets of the
1960's. Detroit: Broadside Press, 1971.

Lerner, Gerda, ed. Black Women in White America. New
York: Pantheon Books, 1972.

Levitt, Kendricks, ed. Afro-American Voices: 1770's-1970's.
New York and Los Angeles: Oxford Book Co., 1970.

Locke, Alain, ed. The New Negro: An Interpretation. Introduction by Allan H. Spear. New York and London:
Johnson Reprint Corp., 1968.

_____, and Montgomery Gregory, eds. Plays of Negro
Life. New York: Harper, 1927.

Lomax, Alan and Raoul Abdu, eds. 3000 Years of Black
Poetry. New York: Dodd, Mead, 1970.

Major, Clarence, ed. New Black Poetry. New York: International Publishers, 1969.

Martin, Jay, ed. A Singer in the Dawn: Reinterpretations of
Paul Laurence Dunbar. New York: Dodd, Mead, 1975.
(Poems, also lectures and papers from the Centenary
Conference on Paul Laurence Dunbar, Fall 1972, Uni-
versity of California, Irvine.)

_____, and Gossie H. Hudson, eds. The Paul Laurence
Dunbar Reader. New York: Dodd, Mead, 1975. (Complete works of Dunbar and other writings, including letters to Alice.)

Miller, Adam David, ed. Dices or Black Bones. Boston:
Houghton Mifflin, 1970.

Mirer, Martin, ed. Modern Black Stories. New York: Bar-
ron's Educational Series, 1971.

Mirikitoni, Janice and others, eds. Time to Greez!

Incantations from the Third World. Introduction by Maya
Angelou. San Francisco: Glide Publications, 1975.

Mitchell, Loften. Black Drama. New York: Hawthorn
Books, Inc. , 1967.

Morgan, Robin, ed. Sisterhood Is Powerful: An Anthology
of Writings from the Women's Liberation Movement.
New York: Random House, 1970.

Nemiroff, Robert, ed. Les Blancs: The Collected Last Plays
of Lorraine Hansberry. Introduction by Julius Lester.
New York: Random House, 1972.

Randall, Dudley, ed. The Black Poets. New York: Bantam,
1971.

Robinson, William H. Early Black American Poets. Dubuque,
Iowa: Wm. C. Brown Co. , 1969.

Rush, Theressa Gunnels, Carol Fairbanks Myers and Esther
Spring Arata. Black American Writers Past and Pre-
sent: A Biographical and Bibliographical Dictionary.
Metuchen, N. J. : Scarecrow, 1975.

Shuman, R. Baird, ed. Nine Black Poets. Durham: Moore
Publishing Co. , 1968.

Singh, Raman K. and Peter Fellowes. Black Literature in
America: A Casebook. New York: Crowell, 1970.

Staples, Robert, ed. The Black Family: Essays and Studies.
Belmont, Calif. : Wadsworth Publishing Co. , 1971.

Thompson, Mary Lou, ed. Voices of the New Feminism.
Boston: Beacon Press, 1971.

Turner, Darwin, ed. Black American Literature: Essays.
Columbus, Ohio: Charles Merrill, 1969.

_____. Black American Literature: Fiction. Columbus,
Ohio: Charles Merrill, 1969.

_____. Black American Literature: Poetry. Columbus,
Ohio: Charles Merrill, 1969.

Vermont Square Writers Workshop. Some Ground to Fall On,

and Other Writings. Los Angeles: Los Angeles Public
Library, under the auspices of the Federal Library Services and Construction Act, 1971.

Watkins, Mel and Jay David. To Be a Black Woman: Portraits in Fact and Fiction. New York: Morrow, 1970.

White, Newman Ivey and Walter Clinton Jackson, eds. An
Anthology of Verse by American Negroes. Durham:
Moore Publishing Co., 1970.

Wilentz, Ted and Tom Weatherly, eds. Natural Process: An
Anthology of New Black Poetry. New York: Hill and
Wang, 1970.

Williams, John A., ed. Beyond the Angry Black. New York:
New American Library, 1966.

c) Collected Works of Individual Black Women

Amini, Johari. Let's Go Somewhere. Chicago: Third World
Press, 1970.

Angelou, Maya. Just Give Me a Cool Drink of Water 'fore I
Die. New York: Random House, 1971.

_____. O Pray My Wings Are Gonna Fit Me Well. New
York: Random House, 1975.

Brooks, Gwendolyn. Family Pictures. Detroit: Broadside
Press, 1970.

_____. Reckonings. Detroit: Broadside Press, 1975.

_____. Riot. Detroit: Broadside Press, 1969.

_____. Selected Poems. New York: Harper & Row, 1963.

_____. The World of Gwendolyn Brooks: A Street in
Bronzeville, Annie Allen, Maud Martha, The Bean Eaters, In the Mecca. New York: Harper, 1971.

Burroughs, Margaret T. G. What Shall I Tell My Children
Who Are Black? Chicago: The Author, 1968.

Clifton, Lucille. Good News About the Earth. New York:
Random House, 1973.

_____. Good Times: Poems. New York: Random House,
1969.

_____. An Ordinary Woman. New York: Random House,
1974.

Clinton, Gloria. Trees Along the Highway. New York:
Comet Press, 1953.

Danner, Margaret. Impressions of African Art Forms. Detroit: Broadside Press, 1968.

Dunbar-Nelson, Alice. The Goodness of St. Roque and Other
Stories. New York: Dodd, Mead, 1899.

_____. Violets and Other Tales. Boston: The Monthly
Review, 1895.

Evans, Mari. I Am a Black Woman. New York: Morrow,
1970.

_____. Where Is All the Music? London: Paul Breman,
Ltd. , 1968.

Fabio, Sarah Webster. A Mirror: A Soul. San Francisco:
Julian Richardson, 1969.

Giovanni, Nikki. Black Feeling, Black Talk, Black Judgment.
New York: Morrow, 1970.

_____. The Women and the Men. New York: Morrow,
1975.

Goss, Clay. Homecookin': Five Plays. Washington: Howard
University Press, 1974.

Grosvenor, Kali. Poems by Kali. Introduction by William
Kelley. Photographs by Joan Halifax and Robert Fletcher. New York: Doubleday, 1966.

Hightower, Ruth. From the Tower: Poetry and Reflections.
New York: Vantage, 1976.

Hunt, Evelyn Tooley. Toad-Song: A Collection of Haiku and

Other Small Poems. New York: Apple Press, 1966.

Ifetayo, Femi Fumni. We The Black Woman. Detroit: Black
Arts Publications, 1970.

Johnson, Georgia Douglas. The Heart of a Woman and Other
Poems. Boston: Cornhill, 1917; reprint, New York:
AMS Press, 1975.

Jones, Lola Amis. Exploring the Black Experience in America: A Bicentennial Edition of Plays and Short Stories:
1976. New York: F. Peters, 1976.

Jordan, June. Some Changes. New York: E. P. Dutton, 1971.

_____. Who Look at Me. New York: Crowell, 1969.

Lane, Pinkie Gordon. Wind Thoughts. Ft. Smith, Ark. :
South and West Publishers, 1972.

Latimore, Jewel C. Images in Black. Chicago: Third World
Press, 1967.

Lorde, Audre. From a Land Where Other People Live. Detroit: Broadside Press, 1973.

Madgett, Naomi Long. One and the Many. New York: Exposition Press, 1956.

_____. Songs to a Phantom Nightingale. New York: For-
tunys, 1941.

_____. Star by Star. Detroit: Harlo Press, 1965.

Mahone, Barbara. Sugarfield Poems. Introduction by Hoyt
W. Fuller. Detroit: Broadside Press, 1970.

Moore, La Nesse B. Can I Be Right? New York: Vantage, 1971.

Murphy, Beatrice and Nancy Arnez. The Rocks Cry Out.
Detroit: Broadside Press, 1969.

Murray, Pauli. Dark Testament and Other Poems. Norwalk,
Conn. : Silvermine, 1970.

Nicholes, Marion. Life Styles. Detroit: Broadside Press, 1971.

Audre Lord.   Photo by Paul Thomas

Petry, Ann. Miss Muriel and Other Stories.   Boston: Houghton Mifflin, 1971.

Ray, Henrietta.   Poems.   New York: Grafton Press, 1910.

Richards, Elizabeth Davis.   The Peddler of Dreams and Other
Poems.   New York: W. A. Bodler, 1928.

Richardson, Nola.   Even in a Maze.   Los Angeles: Crescent
Publications, 1975.

Rodgers, Carolyn M.   How i got ovah: New and Selected
Poems.   New York: Anchor Books, 1976.

_____.   Love Raps.   Chicago: Third World Press, 1969.

_____. Songs of a Black Bird. Chicago: Third World
Press, 1969.

Simms, Lillian. Collection of Poems. Chicago: Lillian
Sims, 1971.

Smith, Sandria. Dria. Long Beach, Calif. : The Author,
1974.

Stephany. Moving Deep. Detroit: Broadside Press, 1969.

Taylor, Gloria Lee. Dreams for Sale. New York: Exposition, 1953.

Thompson, Carolyn. Frank. Detroit: Broadside Press,
1970.

Thompson, Clara Ann. Songs from Wayside. Rossmoyne,
Ohio: The Author, 1900.

Thompson, Dorothenia. Three Slices of Black. Chicago:
Free Black Press, 1972.

Thompson, Priscilla Jane. Ethiope Lays. Rossmoyne, Ohio:
The Author, 1900.

Walker, Alice. In Love and Trouble. New York: Harcourt,
1973.

Walker, Margaret. For My People. New Haven, Conn. :
Yale University Press, 1942.

_____. October Journey. Detroit: Broadside Press, 1973.

_____. Prophets for a New Day. Detroit: Broadside
Press, 1970.

Washington, Mary Helen, ed. Black-Eyed Susans: Classic
Stories by and about Black Women. New York: Anchor,
1975.

Watkins, Violette Peaches. My Dream World of Poetry. New
York: Exposition, 1955.

Watson, Freida K. Feelin's. Introduction by Jomo Don Shabazz. Los Angeles: A Krizna Publication, 1971.

Wheatley, Phillis. Memoir and Poems of Phillis Wheatley:
A Native African and a Slave. Boston: Isaac Knapp,
1938.

_____. The Poems of Phillis Wheatley. Chapel Hill, N.C.:
Julian D. Mason, Jr. , 1966.

6. THE ARTS

Cox, Betty. "Black American Music: The Beginning," Black Art (An International Quarterly) 1:1 (Fall, 1976), 53.

DeKnight, Freda. A Date with a Dish. New York: Hermitage Press, 1970.

Dunham, Katherine. "The Negro Dance." In The Negro Caravan, ed. by Sterling A. Brown and others. New York: Arno Press, 1970.

Fauset, Jessie. "The Gift of Laughter." In Black Expressions, ed. by Addison Gayle. New York: Weybright and Talley, 1969.

George, Zelma Watson. "An Analysis of the Use of Negro Folksong in Six Major Symphonic Works." An unpublished manuscript, 1933.

_____. "Making Use of Negro Thematic Material, Symphonic Works Played by Major Orchestras, 1920-1945." An unpublished manuscript, 1946.

_____. "Negro Music in American Life." In American Negro Reference Book, ed. by John P. Davis. Englewood Cliffs, N. J.: Prentice-Hall, 1966.

Hackley, E. Azalia. A Guide to Voice Culture. Philadelphia: [n. p.], ca. 1909.

Hansberry, Lorraine. "The Negro in the American Theatre." In American Playwright in Drama, ed. by Horst Frenz. New York: Hill and Wang, 1965.

Hare, Maud Cuney. Negro Musicians and Their Music. Washington, D. C.: Associated Publishers, 1936.

Jackson, Peggy. "The Art of Drying Flowers," Essence 2 (March, 1972), 42-43, 65.

Jefferson, Louise E. The Decorative Arts of Africa. New York: Viking, 1973.

Lewis, Edna and Evangeline Peterson. Edna Lewis Cookbook. Indianapolis: Bobbs-Merrill, 1976.

Lewis, Semella and Ruth Woddy. Black Artists on Art. 2 vols. Los Angeles: Contemporary Craft Publishers, 1969, 1971.

McFarland, Ollie and others. Afro-America Sings. Detroit: Board of Education, 1971. (182 pages of songs; also historical and biographical information, pictures, and illustrations).

Montgomery, E[vangeline] J. "Exhibition Chart." Presented at Black Museums Seminar, African-American Historical and Cultural Society, Inc. San Francisco, January 14, 1977.

_____, ed. New Perspectives in Black Art, October 5-26, 1968. Oakland: Oakland Museum Art Division, Kaiser Center Gallery, 1968.

_____. Sargent Johnson, Feb. 23-March 21, 1971. Oakland: Oakland Museum of Art, 1971.

National Council of Negro Women, Inc. The Historical Cook Book of the American Negro. Sue Bailey Thurman, ed. Washington, D. C.: Corporate Press, 1958.

Nicholas, Denise. Beauty Book: A Complete Guide to Good Grooming and Feminine Beauty from Head to Toe. New York: Cornerstone Library, 1971.

Roach, Hildred. Black American Music: Past and Present. Boston: Crescendo Publishing Co., 1973.

Sandler, Joan. "The Black Presence--A Theatre of Creative Alternatives," Black Art (An International Quarterly) 1:1 (Fall, 1976), 40-47.

Schuyler, Philippa Duke. "Music of Modern Africa," Music Journal 18 (October, 1960), 60-63.

Southall, Dr. Geneva. "White Antebellum and Past Emancipa-
tion Attitudes, as Revealed in the 1865 Court Case of
Blind Tom, Musical Genius." Paper presented at the
Association for Negro Life and History, October 18, 1973.

Southern, Eileen. The Music of Black Americans: A History.
New York: W. W. Norton and Co., 1971.

Whiting, Helen Adele. Negro Art and Rhymes. Washington,
D. C.: Associated Publishers, 1963.

_____. Negro Art, Music and Rhyme for Young Folks.
Illus. by Lois Mailou Jones. 2 vols. Washington, D.C.:
Associated Publishers, 1938.

_____. Negro Art, Music, and Rhyme. Illus. by Louis
Mailou Jones. Book II. Washington, D. C.: Associated
Publishers, 1967.

Young, Pauline. "Negro Folk Music and Dancing," Candid
1:6 (November, 1938), 14.

_____. "Negro Popular Music," Candid 1:8 (January,
1939), 14, 15.

7. NOVELS

Banks, Irma Louise. Love in Black and White. New York: Vantage, 1974.

Bellinger, Claudia. Wolf Kitty. New York: Vantage, 1959.

Brooks, Gwendolyn. Maude Martha. New York: Farrar Straus & Giroux, 1969.

Childress, Alice. A Hero Ain't Nothing But a Sandwich. New York: Avon Books, 1973.

_____. Like One of the Family. New York: Independence Publishers, 1956.

DuBois, Shirley Graham. Zulu Heart. New York: The Third Press, 1974.

Dunbar-Nelson, Alice Ruth (Moore). "Confessions of a Lazy Woman." 1901. In the possession of Pauline Young, Wilmington, Delaware. Typewritten.

_____. "This Lofty Oak." Ca. 1931. In the possession of Pauline Young, Wilmington, Delaware. Typewritten.

Fauset, Jessie Redmon. The Chinaberry Tree. New York: Frederick A. Stokes, 1931.

_____. Comedy, American Style. New York: Frederick A. Stokes, 1933. (1969).

_____. Plum Bun. New York: Frederick A. Stokes, 1929.

_____. There Is Confusion. New York: Boni and Livewright, 1924.

Finch, Amanda. Black Trail: A Novella of Love in the South. New York: William-Frederick Press, 1951.

41

Fleming, Sarah Lee Brown. _Hope's Highway_. New York:
  Neale, 1917.

Garrett, Beatrice. _Welfare on Skid Row_. New York: Exposition, 1974.

Greenfield, Eloise. _Sister_. New York: Crowell, 1974.

Guy, Rosa. _Bird At My Window_. Philadelphia: Lippincott,
  1966.

_____. _The Friends_. New York: Holt Rinehart & Win-
  ston, 1973; Viking, 1976.

_____. _Ruby_. New York: Viking, 1976.

Harper, Frances and Ellen Watkins. _Iola LeRoy, or Shadows
  Uplifted_. Philadelphia: Garriques Brothers, 1892.
  (Reprint, New York: AMS Press, 1969.)

Hopkins, Pauline. "Of One Blood: Or the Hidden Self." In
  Colored American Magazine. (Began novel in 1902; it
  ran for twelve installments.)

Hunter, Helen. _Magnificent White Men_. New York: Vantage,
  1964.

Hunter, Kristin. _God Bless the Child_. New York: Scribner,
  1964.

_____. _The Soul Brothers and Sister Lou_. New York:
  Scribner, 1968 (1969).

_____. _The Survivors_. New York: Scribner, 1975.

Hurston, Zora Neale. _Jonah's Gourd Vine_. Philadelphia:
  Lippincott, 1934.

_____. _Moses, Man of the Mountain_. Philadelphia: Lip-
  pincott, 1939.

_____. _Seraph on the Suwanee_. New York: Scribner,
  1948.

_____. _Tell My Horse_. Philadelphia: Lippincott, 1938.

_____. _Their Eyes Were Watching God_. Philadelphia and
  London: Lippincott, 1937 (1969).

Beatrice Garrett

Jones, Gayl. Corregidora. New York: Random House, 1975.

_____. Eva's Man. New York: Random House, 1976.

Jordan, June. His Own Where. New York: Dell, 1971.

Larsen, Nella. Passing. New York and London: Knopf,
    1929.

_____. Quicksand. New York and London: Knopf, 1928.
    (Reprint, New York: Macmillan, 1971.).

Lee, Audrey. The Clarion People. New York: McGraw-Hill,
    1968.

_____. The Workers. New York: McGraw-Hill, 1969.

Marshall, Paule. Brown Girl, Brownstones. New York:
    Random House, 1959.

_____. The Chosen Place, the Timeless People. New
    York: Harcourt, 1969.

Mathis, Sharon Bell. Listen for the Fig Tree. New York:
    Avon, 1975.

Nelson, Annie Greene. After the Storm. Columbia, S. C. :
    Hampton Publishing Co. , 1942.

_____. The Dawn Appears. Columbia, S. C. : Hampton
    Publishing Co. , 1944.

Overstreet, Cleo. The Boar Hog Woman. New York: Double-
    day, 1972.

Petry, Ann. Country Place. Boston: Houghton Mifflin,
    1947.

_____. The Narrows. Boston: Houghton Mifflin, 1953.

_____. The Street. New York: Pyramid Books, 1961.

Polite, Carlene Hatcher. The Flagellants. New York: Far-
    ar, Straus & Giroux, 1967.

_____. Sister X and the Victim of Foul Play. New York:
    Farrar, Straus & Giroux, 1975.

Potter, Valaida. Sunrise over Alabama. New York: Comet
    Press, 1959.

Randall, Florence E. The Almost Years. New York: Athe-
    neum, 1971.

Roberson, Sadie. Killer of the Dream. New York: Carlton
    Press, 1963.

Shaw, Letty M. Angel Mink. New York: Comet Press,
    1957.

Shockley, Ann. Loving Her. Indianapolis: Bobbs-Merrill,
    1974.

Spencer, Mary Etta. The Resentment. Philadelphia: A. M. E.
    Book Concern, 1921.

Vaught, Estella U. Vengeance Is Mine. New York: Comet
    Press, 1959.

Vroman, Mary Elizabeth. Esther. New York: Bantam, 1963.

_____. Harlem Summer. New York: Berkley, 1968.

Alice Walker. Photo by Rhoda Nathans

Walker, Alice. Meridian. New York: Harcourt, 1975; also
    excerpted in Essence (July, 1976), 36-40, 73-78.

_____. The Third Life of Grange Copeland. New York:
    Harcourt, 1970.

Walker, Margaret. Jubilee. Boston: Houghton Mifflin, 1966.

Wallace, Elizabeth West. Scandal at Daybreak. New York:
    Pageant Press, 1954.

Washington, Doris V. Yulan. New York: Carlton Press,
    1964.

West, Dorothy. The Living Is Easy. Boston: Houghton Mif-
    flin, 1948.

Wood, Lillian E. Let My People Go. Philadelphia: A. M. E.
    Book Concern, 1922.

Woods, Odella Phelps. High Ground. New York: Exposition,
    1945.

Wright, Sarah E. This Child's Gonna Live. New York: De-
    lacorte, 1969.

_____, and Lucy Smith. Give Me a Child. Philadelphia:
    Kraft Publishing Co. , 1955.

Wright, Zara. Black and White Tangled Threads. Chicago:
    Privately printed, 1920.

8. PLAYS

Childress, Alice. "Florence: A One-Act Drama," Masses and Mainstream 3 (October, 1950), 34-47.

_____. "Gold Through the Trees." 1952. (Unpublished)

_____. "Just a Little Simple." 1950. (Unpublished)

_____. "Mojo: A Black Love Story," Black World 20:6 (April, 1971), 54-82.

_____. "Trouble in Mind." 1955. (Mimeographed copy in possession of Miss Childress)

_____. Wedding Band. A Love/Hate Story in Black and White. New York: French, 1973.

_____. Wine in the Wilderness. New York: Dramatists Play Service, Inc. , 1969; also in Plays by and about Women, ed. by Victoria Sullivan and James Hatch. New York: Vantage, 1974.

Dunbar-Nelson, Alice. "The Author's Evening at Home," The Smart Set (September, 1900), 105-106.

_____. "Mine Eyes Have Seen." In The Dunbar Speaker and Entertainer, ed. by Alice Dunbar-Nelson. Naperville, Ill. : J. L. Nichols, 1920; also in Black Theater, U. S. A. , Forty-Five Plays by Black Americans, ed. by James V. Hatch. Consultant, Ted Shine. New York: The Free Press, 1974.

Goss, Clay. Homecookin': Five Plays. Washington: Howard Univ. Press, 1974.

Graham, Shirley. Track Thirteen. Boston: Expression Co. , 1940.

47

Grimke, Angelina. Rachel. Boston: Cornhill Co., 1920.

Hansberry, Lorraine. "Les Blancs," "The Drinking Gourd," and "What Use Are Flowers?" In Les Blancs: Collected Last Plays of Lorraine Hansberry, ed. by Robert Nemiroff. New York: Random House, 1972.

_____. A Raisin in the Sun. New York: New American Library, 1959.

_____. The Sign in Sydney Brustein's Window. New York: New American Library, 1966.

_____. To Be Young, Gifted and Black. Adapt. by Robert Nemiroff. Englewood Cliffs, N. J.: Prentice-Hall, 1969.

Hurston, Zora Neale. "The First One: A Play." In Ebony and Topaz, A Collection. Ed. by Charles S. Johnson. New York: National Urban League, 1927.

Jackson, Elaine. "Toe Jam." In Black Drama Anthology, ed. by Woodie King and Ron Milner. New York: Columbia University Press, 1972.

Johnson, Georgia Douglas. "Blue Blood." In Fifty More Contemporary One-Act Plays, ed. by Frank Shay. New York: Appleton, 1928.

_____. "Frederick Douglass." In Negro History in Thirteen Plays, ed. by Richardson. Washington, D. C.: Associated Publishers, 1935.

_____. "Plumes." In Plays of Negro Life, ed. by Alain Locke and Montgomery Gregory. New York: Harper, 1927.

_____. "William and Ellen Craft." In Negro History in Thirteen Plays. Washington, D. C.: Associated Publishers, 1935.

Jones, Lola Amis. Exploring the Black Experience in America: A Bicentennial Edition of Plays and Short Stories: 1976. New York: F. Peters, 1976.

Kennedy, Adrienne. "Funnyhouse of a Negro." In Black Drama: An Anthology, ed. by William Brasmer and

Dominick Consolo. Columbus, Ohio: Charles Merrill, 1970.

_____. "A Rat's Mass." In New Black Playwrights, ed. by William Couch, Jr. Baton Rouge, La. : Louisiana State University Press, 1968.

Meyers, Paulene. "Mama." Performed at Los Angeles, Calif. Studio Theatre Playhouse, May 8-30, 1975.

Moore, Elvie. "Angela Is Happening." Performed in Los Angeles, California, 1971.

Richards, Beah. "Black Woman Speaks." Dramatized, Inner City Cultural Center, Los Angeles, Calif. , 1973.

Salimu. "Growin' into Blackness." In New Plays from the Black Theatre, ed. by Ed Bullins. New York: Bantam, 1969.

Sanchez, Sonia. "Sister Son/Ji." In New Plays from the Black Theatre, ed. by Ed Bullins. New York: Bantam, 1969.

Smith, Jean. "O. C.'s Heart," Black World 6:19 (April, 1970), 56-76.

Spence, Eulalie. Fool's Errand. New York: Samuel French, 1927.

_____. "Help Wanted," Saturday Evening Quill. Boston, 1929.

_____. "The Starter." In Plays of Negro Life. Ed. by Alain Locke and Montgomery Gregory. New York: Harper, 1927.

_____. "Undertow." In Black Theatre, U.S.A. Ed. by James V. Hatch. New York: The Free Press, 1974.

Tillman, Katherine D. Thirty Years After Freedom. [n.p.], [n.d.].

Townsend, Willa A. Because He Lives; A Drama of Resurrection. Nashville: Sunday School Publishers, Board of the National Baptist Convention, 1924.

Wilson, Alice T.   How an American Poet Made Money.   New
York: Pageant, 1968.

9. POEMS

Alvarez, Julia. "Lonely Tulip Grower." In Soulscript, ed. by June Jordan. New York: Doubleday, 1970.

Amini, Johari (Jewel C. Latimore). "Folk Fable." In Black Arts, ed. by Ahmed Alhamisi and Harun Kofi Wangaga. Introduction by Keorapetse Kgoisitsile. Detroit: Black Arts Publications, 1969.

_____. Images in Black. Chicago: Third World Press, 1969.

_____. Let's Go Somewhere. Chicago: Third World Press, 1970.

Angelou, Maya. Just Give Me a Cool Drink of Water 'fore I Die. New York: Random House, 1971.

_____. O Pray My Wings Are Gonna Fit Me Well. New York: Random House, 1975.

Arthur, Barbara. Common Sense Poetry. Berkeley: Respect International Enterprises, 1969.

Avotoja. "A Soulful Sister," Glide In/Out 4 (April, 1972), 1.

Ayo, Zeno. "Investigation." Los Angeles: Author (P.O. Box 77130), 1963.

Bennett, Gwendolyn B. "Hatred" and "Heritage." In American Negro Poetry, ed. by Arna Bontemps. New York: Hill & Wang, 1963.

Bibb, Eloise. Poems. Boston: The Monthly Review Press, 1895.

Bogus, Diane. "Dippity-Did/Done or Can You Do." (To Black

51

Women) In Night Comes Softly, ed. by Nikki Giovanni.
New York: Nik-Tom Publications, 1970.

_____. 'm Off to See the Goddam Wizard, Alright! Chi-
cago: Author, 1971.

Bragg, Linda Brown. A Love Song to Black Men. Detroit:
Broadside Press, 1974.

Brooks, Gwendolyn. Annie Allen. New York: Harper, 1949.

_____. The Bean Eaters. New York: Harper, 1960.

_____. Bronzeville Boys and Girls. New York: Harper,
1956.

_____. Family Pictures. Detroit: Broadside Press, 1970.

_____. "The Life of Lincoln West." In New Writing by
American Negroes, 1940-1962. Selected and edited with
introduction and biographical notes by Herbert Hill.
New York: Knopf, 1968.

_____. "Medgar Evers." In Beyond the Angry Black, ed.
by John A. Williams. New York: New American Library, 1966.

_____. Reckonings. Detroit: Broadside Press, 1975.

_____. Riot. Detroit: Broadside Press, 1969.

_____. Selected Poems. New York: Harper, 1960.

_____. A Street in Bronzeville. New York: Harper,
1945.

_____. "We're the Only Colored People Here." In The
Best Short Stories by Negro Writers, ed. and intro. by
Langston Hughes. Boston: Little, Brown, 1967.

_____. The World of Gwendolyn Brooks: A Street in
Bronzeville, Annie Allen, Maud Martha, The Bean Eaters, In the Mecca. New York: Harper, 1971.

Brown, Mrs. Sarah Lee (Fleming). Clouds and Sunshine.
Boston: The Cornhill Co. , 1920.

Browning, Alice W. , ed. Black n' Blue. Chicago: Browning, n. d.

Burrell, Evelyn Patterson. Weep No More. Philadelphia:
    The Burton Johns Publishing Co. , 1973.

Evelyn Patterson Burrell

Butler, Anna L. Touch Stone. Wilmington, Delaware: Poetry
    Center, 1961.

Chaney, Regina. Brown Sugar: Anthology. Long Beach,
    Calif. : Hwong Publishing Co. , 1974.

_____. My Favorite Things. Long Beach, Calif. : Brown
    Sugar Enterprises, 1976. (A Broadsheet)

Clifford, Carrie. The Widening Light. Boston: Walter Reid
    Co. , 1922.

Clifton, Lucille. Good News About the Earth. New York:
Random House, 1972.

_____. Good Times. New York: Random House, 1970.

_____. An Ordinary Woman. New York: Random House,
1974.

Clinton, Gloria. Trees Along the Highway. New York:
Comet Press, 1953.

Cobb, Pamela. Inside the Devil's Mouth: First Poems.
College Park Station, Detroit: Lotus Press, 1974.

Coleman, Beverly. "The Self-Determination of a Mammy."
In Night Comes Softly, ed. by Nikki Giovanni. New
York: Nik-Tom Publications, 1970.

Collier, Eugenia. "Barbados," Black World 5:25 (March,
1976), 53.

Cumbo, Kattie M. "African Beauty Rose," "Washiri," "Age,"
"All Hung Up," "Domestics," "Another Time, Another
Place," "Bahamas--I," "Bahamas--II," "Black Goddess,"
"Consumed (for Brother Leroi)," "Dark People," "A
Song from Brooklyn," "Malcolm," "Black Sister," and
others. In Nine Black Poets, ed. by R. Baird Shuman.
Durham, N. C. : Moore Publishing Co. , 1968.

Curry, Linda. "Death Prosecuting," and "No Way Out. " In
Soulscript, ed. by June Jordan. New York: Doubleday,
1970.

Danner, Margaret. Impressions of African Art Forms.
Detroit: Braodside Press, 1968.

_____. To Flower. Nashville, Tenn. : Hemphill Press,
1963.

Davis, Gloria. "To Egypt. " In The New Black Poets, ed.
by Clarence Majors. New York: International Publishers, 1969.

Dee, Ruby, ed. Glowchild and Other Poems. New York:
The Third Press, 1972.

Dunbar-Nelson, Alice. "April Is on the Way. " In Ebony and
Topaz. New York: National Urban League, 1927.

Alice Dunbar-Nelson

_____. "Canto--I Sing," The American Interracial Peace
Committee Bulletin, October, 1929.

_____. "Chalmette." In The Dunbar Speaker and Enter-
tainer. Naperville, Ill. : J. L. Nichols, 1920.

_____. "Communion," Opportunity 3:31 (July, 1925), 216.

_____. "Delta Sigma Theta, National Hymn." In The Of-
ficial Ritual of Delta Sigma Theta Grand Chapter.
Washington, D. C. : Delta Sigma Theta Sorority, 1950.

_____. "Forest Fire," Harlem: A Forum of Negro Life
1:1 (November, 1928), 22.

_____. "I Sit and Sew." In Negro Poets and Their
Poems, ed. by Robert Kerlin. Washington, D. C. : Associated Publishers, 1923.

_____. "The Lights at Carney's Point." In The Dunbar
Speaker and Entertainer, ed. by Alice Dunbar-Nelson.
Naperville, Ill. : J. L. Nichols, 1920.

_____. "Music," Opportunity 3:31 (July, 1925), 216.

_____. "Of Old St. Augustine," Opportunity 3:31 (July,
1925), 216.

_____. "Rainy Day," Elmira (New York) Advertiser, Sep-
tember 18, 1898. Alice Dunbar Papers, Ohio Historical
Society (Roll 6, frame 0871).

_____. "Snow in October." In Caroling Dusk, ed. by
Countee Cullen. New York and London: Handy Bros.
Music Co. , 1927.

_____. "Sonnet," also listed as "Violets," Crisis 18:4
(August, 1917), 193.

_____. "Summit and Vale," Lippincott's Magazine 60:420
(December, 1902), 715.

_____. "To Madame Curie," (Philadelphia) Public Ledger,
August 21, 1921.

_____. "To the Negro Farmers of the United States." In
The Dunbar Speaker and Entertainer, ed. by Alice

Dunbar-Nelson. Naperville, Ill. : J. L. Nichols, 1920.

Elliott, Emily. Still Waters and Other Poems. Cambridge:
The Author, 1949.

Evans, Mari. "Coventry," "Status Symbol," "The Emancipa-
tion of George-Hector (A Colored turtle)," "My Man Let
Me Pull Your Coat," "Black Jam for Dr. Negro." In
Black Voices, ed. by Abraham Chapman. New York:
New American Library, 1968.

_____. I Am a Black Woman. New York: Morrow, 1970.

_____. "I'm With You," Negro Digest 17 (May, 1968),
31-36.

_____. Where Is All the Music? London: Paul Breman,
Ltd. , 1968.

Fabio, Sarah. A Mirror: A Soul. San Francisco: Julian
Richardson, 1967.

Fauset, Jessie Redmond. "Christmas Eve in France," "Dead
Firs," "Oriflamme," "Obliviion. " In Book of American
Negro Poetry, ed. by James Weldon Johnson. New
York: Harcourt, 1959.

Faust, Naomi. Speaking in Verse. Boston: Branden Press,
1975.

Fields, Julia. "Alabama Suite, " Black World 4:26 (February,
1975), 40-47.

_____. "A Poem for Heroes," "Boats in Winter," "If Love
Dies," "And Beauty's All Around," "Chopin Deciphered,"
"The Generations," "Eulogy for Philosophers," and
others. In Nine Black Poets, ed. by R. Baird Shuman.
Durham, N. C. : Moore Publishing Co. , 1968.

Ford, Annie L. My Soul Bone Aches. Port Hueneme,
Calif. : Christian Press, 1973.

Fordham, Mary Weston. Magnolia Leaves: Poems. Tuskegee, Alabama: Dept. of Records and Research, 1897.

Giovanni, Nikki. Black Feeling, Black Talk, Black Judgment.
New York: Morrow, 1971.

Annie L. Ford

_____. My House. New York: Morrow, 1972.

_____. The Women and the Men. New York: Morrow,
1975.

Gregory, Carole. "David," "Migration," "NYC Love Poem,"
"Love Poem," "The Cosmic Attack on Poets," "Love
from My Father," "Black Eurydice," "People," and
others. In Nine Black Poets, ed. by R. Baird Shuman.
Durham, N. C. : Moore Publishing Co. , 1968.

Grimke, Angelina W. "Hushed by the Hands of Sleep," "Sur-
render," "When the Green Lies Over the Earth," "A
Winter Twilight." In The Negro Caravan, ed. by Sterling Brown and others. New York: Arno Press, 1970.

_____. "A Mona Lisa." In Black Writers of America,
ed. by Richard Barksdale and Kenneth Kinnamon. New
York: Macmillan, 1972.

Grosvenor, Kali. Poems by Kali. Introduction by William

Melvin Kelley. Photograph by Joan Nalifax and Robert
Fletcher. New York: Doubleday, 1970.

Hansberry, Lorraine. "Flag from a Kitchenette Window,"
Masses and Mainstream 3 (September, 1950), 38-40.

_____. "Lynchsong," Masses and Mainstream 4 (July,
1951), 19-20.

Harper, Frances E. "Bury Me in a Free Land," "Ethiopia,"
"President Lincoln's Proclamation of Freedom," "Fif-
teenth Amendment." In Early Negro American Writers,
ed. by Benjamin Brawley. New York: Dover Press,
Inc. , 1970.

_____. "The Colored People in America (1854)." In Afro
American Voices 1770's-1970's, ed. by Ralph Kendricks
and Claudette Levitt. Los Angeles: Oxford Book Co. ,
1970.

_____. "Eliza," "Bury Me in a Free Land," "Let the
Light Enter," "The Slave Auction." In The Negro Cara-
van, ed. by Sterling Brown and others. New York:
Arno Press, 1970.

_____. Poems on Miscellaneous Subjects. Boston: J. B.
Yerringon and Son, 1854.

_____. "The Slave Auction," "Eliza Harris," "Advice to
the Girls." In Afro American Voices 1770's-1970's, ed.
by Ralph Kendricks and Claudette Levitt. Los Angeles:
Oxford Book Co. , 1970.

_____. The Sparrow's Fall and Other Poems. [n. p.],
[n. d.].

House, Gloria. "Woman," and "Poem." In Black Arts, ed.
by Ahmed Alhamsi and Karun Kofi Wangara. Detroit:
Black Arts Publications, 1969.

Howard, Vanessa. "Reflections," and "Monument in Black."
In Afro American Poetry, ed. by June Jordan. New
York: Doubleday, 1970.

_____. A Screaming Whisper. New York: Holt Rinehart
& Winston, 1972.

[Humphrey], Myrtle Moss. As Much As I Am. Los Angeles:
Capricorn House West, 1973.

_____. "Be a Man ... Boy," "On Love," "Shade of Dif-
ference," "Brother, Take My Hand," "Grits and Gravy."
In Some Ground to Fall On. Los Angeles: Vermont
Square Writers Workshop sponsored by the Los Angeles
Public Library under the auspices of the Federal Library
Services and Construction Act Fund, 1971.

Hunt, Evelyn Tooley. Toad-Song, A Collection of Haiku and
Other Small Poems. New York: Apple Press, 1966.

Ifetayo, Femi Funmi. We the Black Woman. Detroit: Black
Arts Publications, 1970.

Jackson, Mae. Can I Poet with You? New York: Afro-Arts,
1969.

Johnson, Alicia Loy. "Blue/Black Poems (or call them by
their rightful names)," "On My Blk/ness," "A Black
Poetry Day," "The Enemy of Man," "a day of PEACE,
a day of peace," "The Long March." In Nine Black
Poets, ed. by R. Baird Shuman. Durham, N.C.:
Moore Publishing Co., 1968.

Johnson, Dorothy Vena. "Ants," "Escape," "His Smile,"
"Jewels," "Leashed," "Milk," "The Bride," and "To a
Courageous Mother." In Poems for Radio. New York:
Poetry House, 1945.

_____. "Bread for Sale" and "One World." In National
Poetry Anthology of Verse. Written by teachers in
schools and colleges. Los Angeles: National Poetry
Association, 1949.

_____. "Epitaph for a Bigot," "Post War Ballad,"
"Road to Anywhere," and "Success." In Ebony Rhythm,
ed. by Beatrice M. Murphy. New York: Exposition,
1948.

Johnson, Georgia Douglas. An Autumn Love Cycle. New
York: Neal, 1938.

_____. "Black Woman," "Credo," "The Suppliant," "To
William Stanley Braithwaite." In Black American Liter-
ature: Poetry, ed. by Darwin T. Turner. Columbus,
Ohio: Charles Merrill, 1969.

_____. Bronze: A Book of Verse. Boston: Brimmer, 1922.

_____. The Heart of a Woman and Other Poems. Boston: Cornhill, 1917; reprint, New York: AMS Press, 1975.

Johnson, Helene. "The Road," "Poem," "Invocation." In Negro Literature, ed. by Arna Bontemps. New York: Hill & Wang, 1963.

Jones, Gayl. "tripart," "Many Die Here," "Satori." In Soulscript, ed. by June Jordan. New York: Doubleday, 1970.

Jordan, June. New Days: Poems of Exile and Return. New York: Emerson Hall, 1976.

_____. Some Changes. New York: E. P. Dutton, 1971.

_____. Who Look at Me? Illus. with twenty-seven paintings. New York: Crowell, 1969.

_____, ed. Soulscript: Afro-American Poetry. New York: Doubleday, 1970.

Lane, Pinkie Gordon. "Children" and "For Bill," Pembroke Magazine 4 (1973), 26-28.

_____. Discourses in Poetry. 5th Annual Edition. Ft. Smith, Ark. : South and West Publishers, 1972.

_____. "Eulogy on the Death of Trees," Poet: India 5:14 (May, 1973), 477.

_____. "His Body Is an Eloquence." In To Gwen with Love, ed. by Patricia L. Brown and others. Chicago: Johnson Publ. Co. , 1971.

_____. "Mid-Summer Thoughts." In Poems by Poets, Vol. I, ed. by Sue Abbott Boyd. Ft. Smith, Ark: Smith and West Publishers, 1973.

_____. "On This Louisiana Day" and "Poems Extract," Louisiana Review 1:1 (Summer, 1972), 105-106.

_____. "A Quiet Poem." Broadside Series, No. 80. Detroit: Broadside, 1974.

_____. "Reaching" and "Rain Ditch," Journal of Black
Poetry 1:15 (Fall-Winter, 1971), 38-39.

_____. Wind Thoughts. Ft. Smith, Ark.: South and
West Publishers, 1972.

_____, ed. Discourses on Poetry: Prose and Poetry by
Blacks. Vol. 6. Ft. Smith, Ark.: South and West
Publishers, 1972.

_____, ed. Poems by Blacks. Vol. 3. Ft. Smith, Ark.:
South and West Publishers, 1975.

Latimore, Jewel C. Images in Black. Rev. ed. Chicago:
Third World Press, 1967.

Lorde, Audre. Cables to Rage. London: Paul Breman,
1973.

_____. The First Cities. New York: Poets Press, 1967.

_____. From a Land Where Other People Live. Detroit:
Broadside Press, 1973.

_____. "Naturally," "Fantasy and Conversation," "The
Woman Thing," "And What about the Children." In
Natural Process, An Anthology of New Black Poetry,
ed. by Ted Wilentz and Tom Weatherly. New York:
Hill and Wang, 1970.

_____. The New York Head Shop and Museum. Detroit:
Broadside Press, 1971.

_____. "Prologue," Freedomways 12 (First Quarter,
1972), 31.

_____. "Rites of Passage," Freedomways 10 (Third
Quarter, 1970), 246.

McBrown, Gertrude Parthenia. The Picture-Poetry Book.
Illus. by Lois Mailou Jones. Washington: Associated
Publishers, 1968.

Madgett, Naomi. One and the Many. New York: Exposition,
1956.

_____. Songs to a Phantom Nightingale. New York:

Fortuny's, 1941. (Published under the name of Naomi
Cornelia Long.)

_____. Star by Star. Detroit: Harlo Press, 1965.

Mahone, Barbara. Sugarfield Poems. Introduction by Hoyt
W. Fuller. Detroit: Broadside Press, 1970.

Moore, La Nese B. Can I Be Right? New York: Vantage
Press, 1971.

Murphy, Beatrice M. Love Is a Terrible Thing. New York:
Nolsen Book Press, 1945.

_____, and Nancy L. Arnez. The Rocks Cry Out. De-
troit: Broadside Press, 1969.

Murray, Pauli. Dark Testament. Cornstock, Ill. /Norwalk,
Conn. : Silvermine, 1970.

Nicholes, Marion. Life Styles. Detroit: Broadside Press,
1971.

Parker, Patricia. "From Cavities of Bones," "I Followed a
Path," "Assassination. " In Dices or Black Bones, ed.
by Adam David Miller. Boston: Houghton Mifflin, 1970.

Parrish, Dorothy. "Ode to the Uncolored Man," Black Art
Writer's Literary Magazine 1 (First Quarter, 1971), 15.

Quigless, Helen. "Concert. " In The New Black Poetry, ed.
by Clarence Major. New York: International Publishers,
1969.

Rashid, Niema. "Warriors Prancing, Women Dancing. " In
The New Black Poetry, ed. by Clarence Major. New
York: International Publishers, 1969.

Ray, Henrietta Cordella. "Dawn's Carol," "Our Task," "The
Triple Benison. " In An Anthology of Verse by Ameri-
can Negroes, ed. by Newman Ivey White, Walter C.
Jackson and James Hardy Dillard. Durham, N. C. :
Moore Publishing Co. , 1924.

_____. Poems. New York: The Grafton Press, 1910.

Richards, Beah. A Black Woman Speaks. Los Angeles: Inner City Press, 1974.

Richards, Elizabeth Davis. The Peddler of Dreams and Other
    Poems. New York: W. A.' Bodler, 1928.

Richardson, Nola. Even in a Maze. Los Angeles: Crescent
    Publications, 1975.

_____. When One Loves: The Black Experience in Amer-
    ica. Photos by John H. Thompson, Ronald Phillips,
    Roger Lubin. Millbrae, Calif.: Celestial Arts, 1974.

Rodgers, Carolyn. "The Children of Their Sin," Black World
    20 (October, 1971), 78.

_____. how i got ovah: New and Selected Poems by
    Carolyn M. Rodgers. New York: Doubleday (Anchor),
    1976.

_____. "My Lai as Related to No Vietnam Alabama,"
    Black World 19 (September, 1970), 64-65.

_____. Now Ain't That Love. Detroit: Broadside Press,
    1970.

_____. Paper Soul. Chicago: Third World Press, 1968.

_____. Songs of a Black Bird. Chicago: Third World
    Press, 1969.

Sanchez, Sonia. "After Saturday Night Comes Sunday," Black
    World 20:5 (March, 1971), 53-59.

_____. A Blues Book for Blue Black Magical Women.
    Detroit: Broadside Press, 1974.

_____. "For Our Lady." In Natural Process, ed. by
    Ted Wilentz and Tom Weatherly. New York: Hill &
    Wang, 1970.

_____. Home Coming. Detroit: Broadside Press, 1969.

_____. It's A New Day: Poems for Young Brothas and
    Sistuhs. Detroit: Broadside Press, 1971.

_____. We a BaddDD People. Introduction by Dudley
    Randall. Detroit: Broadside Press, 1970.

Shange, Ntozake. "amsterdam avenue/ arsenio/ y tu,"

"toussaint," "cross oceans into my heart," Invisible
City 19-20 (October, 1976), 22-23.

_____. For Colored Girls Who Have Considered Suicide/
When the Rainbow Is Enuf! San Lorenzo, Calif. :
Shameless Hussy Press, 1975.

_____. "on becomin successful," "memory," and "like
the fog & the sun teasin the rapids, " Mademoiselle
(September, 1976), p. 28.

_____ (also Paulette Williams). "Three" (for International
Women's Day), Black Scholar 9:6 (June, 1975), 56-61.

Sims, Lillian. Collection of Poems. Chicago: Lillian Sims
Publisher, 1971.

Spencer, Anne. "Lady, Lady." In The New Negro, ed. by
Alain Locke. New York: Johnson Reprint Corp. , 1968.

_____. "Life-Long, Poor Browning," "At the Carnival,"
"Before the Feast of Shushan," "Line to a Nasturtium."
In The Negro Caravan, ed. by Sterling Brown and others.
New York: Arno Press, 1970.

_____. "Lines to a Nasturtium," and "Letter to My Sis-
ter." In Black Writers of America, ed. by Richard
Barksdale and Kenneth Kinnamon. New York: Macmillan, 1972.

Stephany. Moving Deep. Detroit: Broadside Press, 1969.

Taylor, Gloria Lee. Dreams for Sale. New York: Exposition, 1953.

Terry, Lucy. "Bars of Flight. " In The Black Poets, ed.
by Dudley Randall. New York: Bantam, 1971.

Thomas, Joyce Carol. Blessing. Berkeley: Jacato Press,
1975.

_____. Crystal Breezes. Berkeley: Firesign Press,
1974.

Thompson, Clara Ann. Songs from Wayside. Rossmoyne,
Ohio: The Author, 1908.

Thompson, Priscilla Jane. Ethiope Lays. Rossmoyne, Ohio:
The Author, 1900.

Torres, Brenda. "Catechism," Negro Digest 18:8 (June,
1969), 47.

Walker, Alice. "Facing the Way," "The Abduction of Saints,"
and "Forgiveness," Freedomways 15 (Fourth Quarter,
1975), 265-267.

_____. "Hymn." In Afro-American Literature: An Intro-
duction, ed. by Robert Hayden, David J. Burrows, and
Frederick R. Lapides. New York: Harcourt, 1971.

_____. Once: Poem. New York: Harcourt, 1976.

_____. "Rock Eagle," and "South," Freedomways 11
(Fourth Quarter, 1971), 367-368.

_____. "Talking to My Grandmother Who Died Poor Some
Years Ago (While Listening to Richard Nixon Declare,
'I Am Not a Crook')," Black Scholar 9:6 (June, 1975),
62.

Walker, Margaret. For My People. New Haven, Conn. :
Yale University Press, 1942.

_____. October Journey. Detroit: Broadside Press,
1973.

_____. Prophets for a New Day. Detroit: Broadside
Press, 1970.

Watkins, Violette Peaches. My Dream World of Poetry,
Poems of Imagination, Reality, and Dreams. New York:
Exposition, 1955.

Watson, Freida K. Feelin's. Introduction by Jomo Don Shabazz. Los Angeles: A Krizna Publication, 1971.

Welch, Leona Nicholas. Black Gibraltar. Illus. by Doug
Noble. San Francisco: Leswing Press, 1971.

Wheatley, Phillis. The Poems of Phillis Wheatley. Ed. by
Julian D. Mason, Jr. Chapel Hill: Univ. of N. Carolina Press, 1966.

_____. "To the University of Cambridge in New England,"
"On the Death of the Rev. Mr. George Whitefield," "An
Hymn to the Morning," "An Hymn to the Evening," "On
Imagination," "To S. M. , A Young American Painter on
Seeing His Works," "His Excellency General Washing-
ton," "Liberty and Peace. " In Early Negro American
Writers, ed. by Benjamin Brawley. New York: Dover
Publications, 1970.

Williams, Sherley. The Peacock Poems. Middletown, Conn.:
Wesleyan University Press, 1975.

10. SHORT STORIES

Anderson, Mignon Holland. Mostly Womenfolk and a Man or
Two: A Collection. Chicago: Third World Press,
forthcoming.

Bambara, Toni Cade, ed. Tales and Stories for Black Folks.
New York: Doubleday, 1971.

Banks, Brenda. "Like It Is," Black World 20:8 (June, 1971),
53-57.

Bates, Arthenia. Seeds Beneath the Snow: Vignettes from
the South. Washington, D. C. : Howard University Press,
1975.

Brooks, Gwendolyn. "Lincoln West. " In New Writing by
American Negroes, 1940-1962, selected and edited with
introduction and biographical notes by Herbert Hill.
New York: Knopf, 1968.

Burroughs, Margaret. " 'Strawberry Blonde' That Is, " Black
World 19:9 (July, 1970), 78-81.

Childress, Alice. "The Health Card. " In Harlem, U. S. A. ,
ed. and with introduction by John Henrik Clarke. Berlin: Seven Seas Publishers, 1964.

_____. "I Go to a Funeral. " In Harlem, U. S. A. , ed.
and with introduction by John Henrik Clarke. Berlin:
Seven Seas Publishers, 1964.

Coleman, Wanda. "Watching the Sunset," Black World 4:19
(February, 1970), 53-54.

Collier, Eugenia. "Marigolds," Black World 1:19 (November,
1969), 54-62; also in Brothers and Sisters, ed. by Arnold Adoff. New York: Dell, 1970.

_____. "Sinbad the Cat," Black World 20:9 (July, 1971), 53-55.

Crayton, Pearl. "Cotton Alley." In Brothers and Sisters, ed. by Arnold Adoff. New York: Dell, 1970.

Dunbar-Nelson, Alice Ruth (Moore). "The Ball Dress," Leslie's Weekly 93:2114 (December 12, 1901), n. p.

_____. "Hope Deferred," Crisis 8:15 (September, 1914), 238-242.

_____. "The Little Mother," Brooklyn, New York, Standard Union, March 7, 1900. Paul Laurence Dunbar Papers, Ohio Historical Society (Roll 5, frame 0046).

_____. "The Little Mother," New York Daily News, February 6, 1900.

_____. "Science in Frenchtown--A Short Story," The Saturday Evening Mail, Magazine Section, December 7, 1912, pp. 8-9, 26, 27.

Dunham, Katherine. "Afternoon into the Night." In The Best Short Stories by Negro Writers: An Anthology from 1899 to the Present, ed. by Langston Hughes. Boston: Little, Brown, 1967.

Evans, Mari. JD. New York: Doubleday, 1975.

Fauset, Jessie R. "The Meal." In Afro-American Voices, 1770's-1970's, ed. by Ralph Kendricks and Claudette Levitt. Los Angeles: Oxford Book Co., 1970. (From Chinaberry Tree)

Feelings, Muriel. Jambo Means Hello: Swahilli Alphabet Book. Pictures by Tom Feelings. New York: Dial Press, 1974.

_____. Moja Means One: The Swahilli Counting Book. New York: Dial Press, 1971.

_____. Zomani Goes to Market. New York: Seabury, 1970.

Greenfield, Eloise. "Dream Panoply," Black World 3:19 (January, 1970), 54-58.

_____. "A Tooth for an Eye," Black World 9:19 (July, 1970), 70, 77.

Hunter, Kristin. "Debut." In Black American Literature: Fiction, ed. by Darwin T. Turner. Columbus, Ohio: Charles Merrill, 1969.

Hurston, Zora N. "Sweat." In Black American Literature: Fiction, ed. by Darwin T. Turner. Columbus, Ohio: Charles Merrill, 1969.

Jackson, Mae. "I Remeber Omar," Black World 18:8 (June, 1969), 83-85.

Jones, Gayl. "Spaces," Black Scholar 9:6 (June, 1975), 53-55.

Jones, Lois Amis. "Buddy: A Portrait in Black," and "Till Fen Comes Back." In Exploring the Black Experience in America. New York: F. Peters, 1976.

Lee, Audrey. "Alienation," Black World 21:1 (November 1971), 64-66.

_____. "The Black," Black World 12:19 (October, 1970), 64-72.

_____. "I'm Going to Move Out of This Emotional Ghetto," Black World 2:19 (December, 1969), 63-68.

_____. "Moma," Black World 4:18 (February, 1969), 64-65.

Marshall, Paule. "Reena," Harper's Magazine 335 (October, 1962), 154-164; also in The Black Woman, ed. by Toni Cade. New York: NAL, 1970; and in Black-Eyed Susans, ed. by Mary Helen Washington. New York: Doubleday, 1975.

_____. "Some Get Wasted." In Harlem, U.S.A., ed. and with Introduction by John Henrik Clarke. Berlin: Seven Seas Publishers, 1964.

Moody, Anne. Mr. Death: Four Stories. New York: Harper, 1975.

Oliver, Diane. "Neighbors." In Black Voices, ed. by Abraham Chapman. New York: New American

Library (Mentor), 1968.

Petry, Ann. "In Darkness and Confusion." In Black Voices,
    ed. by Abraham Chapman. New York: New American
    Library (Mentor), 1968.

_____. Miss Muriel and Other Stories. Boston: Hough-
    ton Mifflin, 1971.

Rodgers, Carolyn. "A Statistic Trying to Make It Home,"
    Black World 18:8 (June, 1969), 68-71.

Sanchez, Sonia. We Be Word Sorcerers: 25 Stories by Black
    Americans. New York: Bantam, 1973.

Shockley, Ann Allen. "Is She Relevant?" Black World 15:3
    (January, 1971), 58-65.

_____. "To Be a Man," Black World 18:9 (July, 1969),
    54-65.

Smith, Jean. "Something-to-Eat," Black World 20:8 (June,
    1971), 70-76.

Vroman, Mary Elizabeth. "See How They Run." In The
    Best Short Stories by Negro Writers, ed. and Introduc-
    tion by Langston Hughes. Boston: Little, Brown, 1967.

Walker, Alice. "To Hell with Dying." In The Best Short
    Stories by Negro Writers: An Anthology from 1899 to
    the Present, ed. and introduction by Langston Hughes.
    Boston: Little, Brown, 1967.

_____. "The Welcome Table," Freedomways 10 (Third
    Quarter, 1970), 242-246.

West, Dorothy. "The Richer, the Poorer." In The Best
    Short Stories by Negro Writers, ed. and introduction by
    Langston Hughes. Boston: Little, Brown, 1967.

Young, Carrie Allen. "Adjoo Means Goodbye." In Beyond the
    Angry Black, ed. by John A. Williams. New York:
    New American Library, 1966.

11. BOOKS FOR YOUNG READERS

Baker, Augusta. The Golden Lynx and Other Tales. Illustrated by Johannes Troyer. Philadelphia: Lippincott, 1960.

_____. The Talking Tree. Illustrated by Johannes Troyer. Philadelphia: Lippincott, 1955.

Bond, Jean Carey. Brown Is a Beautiful Color. Illustrated by Barbara Zuber. New York: Franklin Watts, 1972.

Brooks, Gwendolyn. The Tiger Who Wore White Gloves or What You Are You Are. Chicago: Third World Press, 1974.

Burroughs, Margaret Taylor. Jasper the Drummin' Boy. Illustrated by Ted Lewin. Chicago: Follett Publishing Co. , 1970.

Chambers, Lucille Arcola. Negro Pioneers: Benjamin Banneker, Mathematician and Astronomer. Art by John Neal. New York: C & S Ventures (G. P. O. Box 209), 1970.

Clifton, Lucille. The Black BC's. Illustrated by Don Miller. New York: E. P. Dutton, 1970.

_____. Don't You Remember? New York: Dutton, 1973.

_____. Everett Anderson's Christmas Coming. New York: Holt Rinehart & Winston, 1972.

_____. Everett Anderson's Friend. Illustrated by Ann Grifalconi. New York: Holt Rinehart & Winston, 1976.

_____. Some of the Days of Everett Anderson. Illustrated by Evaline Ness. New York: Holt Rinehart & Winston, 1970.

_____. The Times They Used to Be. New York: Holt
Rinehart & Winston, 1974.

Giovanni, Nikki. Ego Tripping and Other Poems for Young
People. Illustrated by George Ford. Westport, Conn.:
Laurence Hill, 1974.

Greenfield, Eloise. Bubbles. Illustrated by Eric Marlow.
Washington, D. C. : Drum and Spear, 1972.

_____. Me and Nessie. Illustrated by Moreta Barnett.
New York: Crowell, 1975.

_____. "Rosa Parks," MS 3:2 (August, 1974), 71-74.

_____. She Come Bringing Me That Little Baby Girl.
Philadelphia: Lippincott, 1974.

_____. Sister. New York: Crowell, 1974.

Guy, Rosa. The Friends. New York: Holt Rinehart & Winston, 1973; Viking, 1976.

_____, ed. Children of Longing. New York: Bantam,
1971.

Hamilton, Virginia. The House of Dies Drear. New York:
Macmillan, 1968.

_____. M. C. Higgins, the Great. New York: Macmil-
lan, 1970.

_____. The Planet of Junior Brown. New York: Mac-
millan, 1970.

_____. The Time-Ago Tales of Jahdu. New York: Mac-
millan, 1969.

_____. W. E. B. DuBois: A Biography. New York:
Crowell, 1972.

_____. Zeely. New York: Macmillan, 1967.

Holt, Delores L. The ABC's of Black History. Illustrated
by Samuel Bhang. Los Angeles: The Ward Ritchie
Press, 1971; reprint, 1973.

Hunter, Kristin. Boss Cat. New York: Scribner, 1971; reprint, Avon, 1975.

_____. Guest in the Promised Land. New York: Scrib-
ner, 1973.

Jackson, Florence. The Black Man in America, 1791-1861.
New York: Franklin Watts, 1971. (Grade 7 up)

_____. The Black Man in America, 1861-1877. New
York: Franklin Watts, 1971. (Grades 4-6)

_____. The Black Man in America, 1877-1905. New
York: Franklin Watts, 1973. (Grade 5 up)

_____. The Black Man in America, 1905-1932. New York:
Franklin Watts, 1974. (Grade 7 up)

_____. The Black Man in America, 1932-1954. New York:
Franklin Watts, 1974. (Grades 4-6)

Johnson, Nelle. The Wisdom of an Owl. Los Angeles: At-
lantic-Richfield and others, 1975. Available from Vernon Branch, Los Angeles Public Library. (Author was
aunt of Ralph Bunche.)

Jordan, June. His Own Where. New York: Dell, 1971;
Laurel, 1973.

King, Helen H. Willy. Pictures by Carole Byard. New
York: Doubleday, 1971.

Landrum, Bessie. Stories of Black Folk for Little Folk.
Atlanta, Ga.: A. B. Caldwell Publishing Co., 1923.

Mathis, Sharon. The Hundred Penny Box. New York: Viking,
1975.

_____. Ray Charles. Ed. by Susan Weber. New York:
Crowell, 1973.

_____. The Sidewalk Story. New York: Viking, 1971.

_____. Teacup Full of Roses. New York: Viking, 1972.

Meriwether, Louise. The Freedom Ship of Robert Smalls.
Illustrated by Lee Jack Morton. Englewood Cliffs, N.J.:
Prentice-Hall, 1971.

Petry, Ann. Legends of the Saints. New York: Crowell,
1970.

_____. Tituba of Salem Village. New York: Crowell,
1964.

Rollins, Charlemae Hill. Black Troubador: Langston Hughes.
New York: Rand McNally, 1949.

_____. Christmas Gif'. Line drawings by Tom O'Sullivan.
Chicago: Follett Publishers, 1963.

Tarry, Ellen. Janie Belle. Illustrated by Myrtle Sheldon.
New York: Garden City Publishing Co., 1940.

_____. Katharine Drexel, Friend of the Neglected. Illus-
trated by Donald Bolognese. New York: Farrar Straus
& Cudahy, 1950.

_____. The Runaway Elephant. Pictures by Oliver Har-
rington. New York: Viking, 1950.

_____. Young Jim: The Early Years of James Weldon
Johnson. New York: Dodd, Mead, 1967.

Taylor, Mildred. Song of the Trees. New York: Dial, 1975.

Turner, Mae Caeser. Uncle Ezra Holds Prayer Meeting in
the White House. New York: Exposition, 1970.

Vroman, Mary Elizabeth. Harlem Summer. Illustrated by
John Martines. New York: Putnam, 1967.

Walker, Mildred Pitts. Lillie of Watts Takes a Giant Step.
Illustrated by Bonnie Helene Johnson. Garden City,
N.Y.: Doubleday, 1971.

Watson, Willie Mae. Martin Luther King. Frontispiece,
Persis Jennings. Syracuse, N.Y.: New Readers Press,
1968.

Wilson, Beth. The Great Menu. Chicago: Follett, 1974.

_____. Muhammad Ali. New ed. New York: Putnam,
1974.

12.   THE FOLK TRADITION

Brooks, Gwendolyn. "At the Royal" and "Of DeWitt Williams on His Way to Lincoln Cemetery."   In Book of Negro Folklore, ed. by Langston Hughes and Arna Bontemps. New York: Dodd, Mead, 1958.

Dunham, Katherine. "The Negro Dance."   In The Negro Caravan, ed. by Sterling Brown and others.   New York: Arno Press, 1970.

George, Zelma Watson. "An Analysis of the Use of Negro Folksong in Six Major Symphonic Works."   An unpublished manuscript, 1933.

Hurston, Zora Neale. Jonah's Gourd Vine. Philadelphia: Lippincott, 1934.

_____. Moses, Man of the Mountain. Philadelphia: Lippincott, 1939.

_____. Mules and Men. Philadelphia: Lippincott, 1935; reprint, New York: First Perennial Library Edition, Harper, 1970.

_____. "Polk County, A Comedy of Negro Life on a Sawmill Camp."   Unpublished manuscript, n. d.

_____. "Spunk."   In The New Negro, ed. by Alain Locke. New York: Johnson Reprint Corp. , 1968.

_____. "Sweat."   In Black American Literature: Fiction, ed. by Darwin Turner.   Columbus, Ohio: Charles Merrill, 1969.

_____. Tell My Horse. Philadelphia: Lippincott, 1938.

_____. Their Eyes Were Watching God. Greenwich, Conn. : Fawcett, 1935; Philadelphia: Lippincott, 1937.

Lewis, Dr. Samella.   "The Street Art of Black America,"
    Exxon, U. S. A. (Third Quarter, 1972), 2-9.

Walker, Margaret.   "Molly Means."   In Book of Negro Folk-
    lore, ed. by Langston Hughes and Arna Bontemps.   New
    York: Dodd, Mead, 1958.

Whiting, Helen Adele.   Negro Folk Tales for Pupils in the
    Primary Grades.   Illustrated by Lois Mailou Jones.
    Book I.   Washington, D. C. : Associated Publishers,
    1938.

13. CRITICISM BY BLACK WOMEN

Amini, Johari. "Big Time Buck White," Black World 20:12 (October, 1971), 72-74.

Arnez, Nancy L. "Racial Understanding Through Literature," English Journal 58 (January, 1969), 56-61.

Baker, Augusta. The Black Experience in Children's Books. New York: New York Public Library, 1963.

Bond, Jean Carey. Keeping the Faith: Writings by Contemporary Black American Women, ed. by Pat Crutchfield Exum. Greenwich, Conn. : Fawcett Publications. In Freedomways 15 (Second Quarter, 1975), 125.

Brooks, Gwendolyn. A Capsule Course in Black Poetry Writing. Detroit: Broadside Press, 1975.

Christian, Barbara. An Ordinary Woman. Poems by Lucille Clifton. New York: Random House, 1974. In Black Scholar 1:7 (September, 1975), 52-54.

Collier, Eugenia. "Ain't Supposed to Die a Natural Death," Black World 6:21 (April, 1972), 79-81.

Cuney-Hare, Maud. Negro Musicians and Their Music. Washington, D. C. : Associated Publishers, 1936; reprint, DaCapo Press, 1974.

Dee, Ruby. "Exciting Novel by Talented Story Teller." Review of The Autobiography of Miss Jane Pittman, by Ernest J. Gaines. New York: Dial Press; Freedomways 11 (Second Quarter, 1971), 202-203.

_____. "The Tattered Queens," Negro Digest 15:6 (April, 1966), 32-36.

Dunbar-Nelson, Alice Ruth (Moore). "An Artist in the Family," by Sarah Gertrude Millin. Pittsburgh Courier, February 27, 1930, p. 6.

_____. "Blind Spots," by Henry Smith Leiper. Pittsburgh Courier, February 1, 1930, p. 6.

_____. Bronze: A Book of Verse, by Georgia Douglass Johnson. Introduction by W. E. B. DuBois. Boston: B. J. Brimmer Co. Reviewed by Alice Dunbar-Nelson in The Messenger 5:5 (May, 1923), 698, 719.

_____. "Negro Literature for Negro Pupils," The Southern Workman 51:2 (February, 1922), 59-63.

_____. "Not Without Laughter." The Eagle--National News of the I. B. P. O. E. , Friday, 1930; also in the Washington Tribune.

_____. "Wordsworth's Use of Milton's Description of the Building of Pandemonium." Letter in Modern Language Notes 24:4 (April, 1909), 124-125.

_____, and others. Paul Laurence Dunbar: Poet Laureate of the Negro Race. Philadelphia: A. M. E. Church Review, 1914.

Dunham, Katherine. "The Negro Dance." The Negro Caravan, ed. by Sterling Brown and others. New York: Arno Press, 1970.

Fabio, Sarah. "A Black Paper: An Essay on Literature," Negro Digest 18:9 (July, 1969), 26-29.

_____. "Tripping with Black Writing." In The Black Aesthetic, ed. by Addison Gayle. Garden City, N. Y. : Doubleday, 1971.

Fields, Julia. "The Green of Langston's Ivy," Negro Digest 16:11 (September, 1967), 58-59.

Gant, Liz. "Les Blancs, by Lorraine Hansberry." In Black World 6:20 (April, 1971), 46-47.

Garland, Phyl. "The Prize Winners, Vastly Different New York Plays Bring Top Awards to Blacks," Ebony 25:7 (July, 1970), 29-37.

George, Zelma. "Negro Music in American Life." In The American Negro Reference Book, ed. by John P. Davis. Englewood Cliffs, N. J. : Prentice-Hall, 1966.

Giovanni, Nikki. "Black Poems, Poseurs and Power," Negro Digest 28:8 (June, 1969), 30-34.

_____. "The Chosen Place, the Chosen People, by Paule Marshall." In Black World 3:19 (January, 1970), 51-52, 84.

Handy, Antoinette. Black Music: Opinions and Reviews. Introduction by Edgar A. Toppin. Ettrick, Va. : BM & M (P. O. Box 103), [n. d.].

Hansberry, Lorraine. "Genet, Mailer and the New Paternalism," Village Voice, June 1, 1961, pp. 10-15.

_____. "A Letter from Lorraine Hansberry on Porgy and Bess," The Theater, August, 1959, p. 10.

_____. "Me Tink Me Hear Sounds in De Night." In American Playwrights on Drama, ed. by Horst Frenz. New York: Hill & Wang, 1965.

Harris, Jessica. "An Interview with Alice Walker," Essence (July, 1976), 33.

Harris, Trudier. "Violence in 'The Third Life of Grange Copeland,'" CLA Journal 2:19 (December, 1975), 238-247.

Hull, Gloria T. "A Note on the Poetic Technique of Gwendolyn Brooks," CLA Journal 2:19 (December, 1975), 280-285.

Hutson, Jean S. Blackwell. "Choosing Books for Harlemites," Opportunity 17:5 (May, 1939), 146-148.

Jackson, Esther Merle. "The American Negro and the Image of the Absurd," Phylon: The Atlanta University Review of Race and Culture 23 (Winter, 1962), 359-371.

Jackson-Brown, Irene V. "Afro-American Song in the Nineteenth Century: A Neglected Source," Black Perspectives in Music 1:4 (Spring, 1976), 23-38.

Johnson, Helen Armstead. "Ododo," by Joseph A. Walker, Black World 6:20 (April, 1971), 47-48.

Jordan, June. "On Richard Wright and Zora Neale Hurston: Notes Toward a Balancing of Love and Hatred," Black World 13:10 (August, 1974), 4-8.

Kennedy, Janie Sykes. Brown Gal in de Ring. Collected and arranged by Olive Lewin. London: Oxford University Press, 1974; in Black Perspectives in Music 3:3 (Fall, 1975), 340-341.

McGinty, Doris. Ethnomusicology: U. S. Black Music Issue 19 (September, 1975), ed. by Portia K. Maultsby (guest) and Gerard Behague. In Black Perspectives in Music 1:4 (Spring, 1976), 117-118.

Marsh, Vivian Osborne. "Origin and Distribution of Negro Folklore in America." Masters thesis, University of California, Berkeley, 1921.

Maultby, Portia K. "Music of Northern Independent Churches During the Ante-Bellum Period," Ethnomusicology 3:19 (September, 1975), 401-402.

Nicholas, Denise. "Blacks in Television," Black World 6:25 (April, 1976), 36-42.

Petry, Ann (Lane). "The Novel in Social Criticism." In The Writer's Book, ed. by Helen Rose. Presented by the Author's Guild. New York: Harper, 1950.

Rogers, Norma. "To Destroy Life." Review of A Hero Ain't Nothing But a Sandwich, by Alice Childress. New York: Coward, McCann and Geoghegan. In Freedomways 1:14 (First Quarter, 1974), 72-75.

Rushing, Andrea Benton. "The Changing Same: Images of Black Women in Afro-American Poetry," Black World 11:24 (September, 1975), 18-30.

Smith, Barbara. "Beautiful, Needed, Mysterious." Review of Sula by Toni Morrison. New York: Alfred A. Knopf. In Freedomways 14 (First Quarter, 1974), 72-75.

Smith, Jessie Carnie. "Developing Collections of Black Literature," Black World 20:8 (June, 1971), 18-29.

Smitherman, Geneva. "Ron Milner, People's Playwright,"
Black World 6:25 (April, 1976), 4-19.

Southerland, Ellease. "Zora Neale Hurston: The Novelist-
Anthropologist's Life/Works," Black World 23:10 (August, 1974), 20-30.

Teer, Barbara Ann. "Needed: A New Image." In The Black
Power Revolt, ed. by Floyd Barbour. Boston: Porter
Sargent, 1968.

Walker, Alice. "A Writer Because of, Not in Spite of, Her
Children." In Second Class Citizen, by Buchi Emecheta.
New York: George Braziller. In MS. 2:4 (January,
1976), 40, 106.

Walker, Margaret. How I Wrote "Jubilee." Chicago: Third
World Press, 1972.

_____. "The Shaping of Black America," by Luane Ben-
nett. In Freedomways 15 (Fourth Quarter, 1975),
280-282.

Washington, Mary Helen. "Black Women Image Makers,"
Black World 10:23 (August, 1974), 10-18.

Williams, Ruby Ora. "An In-Depth Portrait of Alice Dunbar-
Nelson." Dissertation, microfilm or xerographic copies.
Ann Arbor: Xerox UM, 1974.

Williams, Sherley. Give Birth to Brightness. New York:
Dial, 1972.

14: MISCELLANEOUS SUBJECTS:

Cultural, Educational, Political,
Social, Racial

Alston, Fannie and R. Ora Williams. "Johnny Doesn't/Didn't
Hear," Journal of Negro Education 33 (Spring, 1864),
197-200.

Amini, Johari. "Re-definition: Concept As Being," Black
World 21:7 (May, 1972), 4-12.

Arnez, Nancy L. "A Study of Attitudes of Negro Teachers
and Pupils Toward Their School," Journal of Negro
Education 32 (Summer, 1963), 289-293.

_____, and Clara Anthony. "Working with Disadvantaged
Negro Youth in Urban Schools," School and Society 96
(March 20, 1968), 202-204.

Austin, Elsie. "Casenotes," University of Cincinnati Law
Review, 1928.

Bass, Charlotta A. Forty Years: Memoirs from the Pages
of a Newspaper. Los Angeles: Charlotta A. Bass,
1960.

Bethune, Mary McLeod. "The Problems of the City Dweller,"
Opportunity 26:3 (February, 1925), 54-55.

Blaylock, Enid. "Article 3.3: California's Answer to Cultural Diversity in the Classroom," Phi Delta Kappan
(November, 1975).

Bowen, Uvelia S. A. Housekeeping Careers--A New Fron-
tier. Philadelphia: Heart, 1973.

_____. Rhyme, Reason and Responsibility. Philadelphia:
Heart, 1971. (Manual)

83

_____. Training Household Technicians. Philadelphia:
Heart, 1971.

_____. What Is a Day's Work? Philadelphia: Personnel
Resources, Inc. , 1970.

_____, Betty Henken and Laura Lee. Thursday's People
on the Move! Philadelphia: Heart, 1971.

Bradley, Gladyce N. "Teacher Education and Desegregation,"
Journal of Negro Education 26 (Spring, 1957), 200-203.

Brown, Charlotte Hawkins. "Morning," an Appeal to the
Heart of the South. Boston: The Philgrim Press, 1919.

Bruce, Beverlee. "Afro-Americans and Language," Ufahamu:
Journal of the African Activist Association 1 (Fall, 1970),
63-67.

Butcher, Margaret Just. The Negro in American Culture.
Rev. and updated edition. Based on materials of Alain
Locke. New York: NAL, 1956.

Butts, Trudi, Betty S. Williams, and Kathy Hedicke, eds.
Care of the Geriatric Patient. A Manual for the Nurse
Aide. Washington D.C.: Department of Health, Educa-
tion, and Welfare, Health Resources Administration, n. d.

Carroll, Constance M. "Yet Another Slice of Pie. " Paper
read at the United States Office of Education Summer
Institute, Challenge: Women in Higher Education. University of California, Irvine, June 25-July 1, 1972.

Cooper, June M. "Training of Teachers of Speech for the
Economically Disadvantaged Black American Student,"
Western Speech (Spring, 1970), 139-143.

Curry, Gladys J. "Black Politics: A Brief Survey. " In
Viewpoints from Black America, ed. by Gladys J. Curry.
Englewood Cliffs, N.J. : Prentice-Hall, 1970.

Dansby, Pearl Gore. "Black Pride in the Seventies: Fact
or Fantasy?" Black Psychology, ed. by Reginald L.
Jones. New York: Harper, 1972.

Davis, Angela. "Political Prisoners, Prisons, and Black Liberation. " In If They Come in the Morning, ed. by Angela

Uvelia S. A. Bowen

Davis and Bettina Apthecker. New York: Joseph A.
Opaku, Inc. , 1971.

_____. "Reflections on the Black Woman's Role in the
Community of Slaves," Black Scholar 3 (December,
1971), 3-15.

DuBois, Shirley Graham. "Egypt Is Africa. " Part 1. Black
Scholar 1 (May, 1970), 20-22.

_____. "Egypt Is Africa. " Part 2. Black Scholar 2
(September, 1970), 28-34.

_____. "The Liberation of Africa," Black Scholar 2 (Feb-
ruary, 1971), 32-37.

_____. "The Struggle in Lesotho, " Black Scholar 2 (No-
vember, 1970), 25-39.

Dunbar-Nelson, Alice Ruth (Moore). "The Boys of Howard High. "
In The Dunbar Speaker and Entertainer, ed. by Alice Dunbar-Nelson. Naperville, Ill.: J. L. Nichols, 1920.

_____. "Is It Time for the Negro Colleges in the South
to Be Put in the Hands of Negro Teachers?" In The
American Negro, His History and Literature, ed. by
D. W. Culp. New York: Arno Press, 1969.

_____. "Training Teachers of English," Education 29
(October, 1908), 97-103.

_____, and others. Untitled anti-lynching statement drafted
in 1922 in support of the NAACP campaign. In Black
Women in White America, ed. by Gerda Lerner. New
York: Random House (Vintage), 1973.

George, Zelma Watson. "The Social Conditions of Slavery
as Found in Slave Narratives. " Unpublished manuscript,
1946.

Giovanni, Nikki, and Margaret Walker. A Poetic Equation:
Conversations Between Nikki Giovanni and Margaret
Walker. Washington, D.C.: Howard University Press,
1974.

Goff, Regina Mary. Problems and Emotional Difficulties of
Negro Children as Studied in Selected Communities and

Attributed by Parents and Children to the Fact that They Are Negro.... New York: Bureau of Publications, Columbia University, 1949.

Gresham, Jewell Handy. "The Rockefeller-Albert Snafu and the Honor of Ed Brooks," New York Amsterdam News, Sunday, October 2, 1976, p. 1.

Guzman, Jessie Parkhurst. Desegregation and the Southern States, 1957. Legal Action and Voluntary Group Action. With Woodrow W. Hall. Tuskegee Institute, Alabama: DRR, 1958.

_____. "Meeting the Social Needs of Students at Tuskegee Institute," The Quarterly Review of Higher Education Among Negroes 12 (October, 1944), 227-231.

_____. The New South and Higher Education. A Symposium and Ceremonies Held in Connection with the Inauguration of Luther Hilton Foster, Fourth President of Tuskegee Institute. Tuskegee Institute, Alabama: DRR, 1954.

_____. "The Role of the Black Mammy in the Plantation Household," Journal of Negro History 23 (July, 1938), 239-69.

_____. "The Social Contributions of the Negro Woman Since 1940," Negro History Bulletin 11 (January, 1948), 86-94.

_____. Some Achievements of the Negro Through Education. Tuskegee, Alabama: DRR, 1954.

_____. "The Southern Race Problem in Retrospect," Vital Speeches 25 (July 1, 1959), 566-568.

_____. Tuskegee Institute Conference on the Disadvantaged. Held in Conjunction with the Annual Meeting of the Tuskegee Institute Board of Trustees, October 25-26, 1964. Tuskegee Institute, Alabama: Tuskegee Institute Press, 1964.

_____. "Twenty Years of Court Decisions Affecting Higher Education in the South, 1938-1958," Journal of Educational Sociology 22 (February, 1958), 247-253.

88   American Black Women

_____. Twenty Years of Court Decisions Affecting Higher
Education in the South. Tuskegee Institute, Alabama:
DRR, 1960.

_____, ed. Race Relations in the South. Tuskegee Insti-
tute, Alabama: DRR, 1956-1964.

Hansberry, Lorraine. "A Challenge to Artists." Speech advocating the abolition of the House UnAmerican Activities
Committee. In Freedomways 3 (Winter, 1963), 33-35.

_____. "Congolese Patriot." Letter to the editor. New
York Times Magazine, March 26, 1961, p. 4.

_____. The Movement: The Documentary of a Struggle
for Equality. New York: Simon and Schuster, 1964.

_____. "Negroes and Africa." Quoted extensively in this
chapter in The New World of Negro Americans, ed. by
Harold R. Isaacs. New York: John Day Co., 1965.

Harris, Janet. Students in Revolt. New York: McGraw-
Hill, 1970.

Haynes, Carrie Ayers. Good News on Grape Street: The
Transformation of a Ghetto School. New York: Citation
Press, 1975.

Height, Dorothy. America's Promise. New York: Woman's
Press, 1946.

_____. The Core of America's Race Problem. New York:
Woman's Press, 1945.

_____. Step by Step with.... Rev. ed. New York: Na-
tional Board YWCA, Publishing Services, 1955.

Hobson, Sheila Smith. "Women and Television." In Sisterhood Is Powerful, ed. by Robin Morgan. New York:
Random House (Vintage), 1970.

Hurston, Zora Neale. "I Saw Negro Votes Peddled," American Legion Magazine (November, 1950), 12-13, 45-46,
59-60.

_____. "A Negro Voter Sizes Up Taft," Saturday Evening
Post 234 (December 8, 1951), 150-152.

_____. "What White Publishers Won't Print," Negro Digest 5:6 (April, 1947), 85-89.

Jackson, Jacqueline J. "Aged Blacks: A Potpourri in the Direction of Reduction of Inequities," Phylon 32 (Third Quarter, Fall, 1971), 260-280.

_____. "A Black Sociologist Crystallizes Social and Psychological Needs to the Characteristics and Special Problems of Ghetto Youth." In Multimedia Materials for Afro-American Studies: A Curriculum Orientation and Annotated Bibliography of Resources, ed. and compiled by Dr. Harry A. Johnson. New York: R. R. Bowker, 1971.

_____. "Where Are the Black Men?" Ebony 27:8 (March, 1972), 99-102, 104, 106.

"Joanne Little: America Goes on Trial," Editorial in Freedomways 15 (Second Quarter, 1975), 87-88.

Johnson, Patricia Ann. "Intellectual Genocide," Black World 10:23 (August, 1974), 81-82.

McFarlin, Anjennette Sophie. Black Congressional Reconstruction: Orators and Their Orations. Metuchen, N.J.: Scarecrow, 1976.

Matthews, Mirriam and Mary Murdoch. "Weeding and Replacement." Paper presented at the University of Southern California workshop on "Improving the Book Collection," March, 1959.

Mosby, Doris P. "Toward a New Speciality of Black Psychology." In Black Psychology, ed. by Reginald L. Jones. New York: Harper, 1972.

_____. "Toward a Theory of the Unique Personality of Blacks--A Psychocultural Assessment." In Black Psychology, ed. by Reginald L. Jones. New York: Harper, 1972.

Moseley, Vivian H. and Dolorise B. Ashley. Unique Bulletin Board Ideas. Illustrated by S. L. Mindingall, Jr. Los Angeles: Precision Printers, 1964.

Musgrave, Marian E. "Teaching English as a Foregin

Language to Students with Sub-Standard Dialects." In
Viewpoints from Black America, ed. by Gladys J. Curry.
Englewood Cliffs. : Prentice-Hall, 1970.

Noble, Jeanne. The Negro Woman's College Education. New
York: Columbia Teachers College, 1975.

_____. "Negro Women Today and Their Education," Jour-
nal of Negro Education 26 (Winter, 1957), 15-21.

Saunders, Doris E. The Kennedy Years and the Negro.
Chicago: Johnson Publ. Co. , 1954.

Schuyler, Philippa. Who Killed the Congo? New York: Devin-Adair Co. , 1962.

Smalley, Hazel C. "Quiet Experiment in Public Affairs,"
Black Politician 2 (January, 1971), 26, 27.

Smith, Jean. "I Learned to Feel Black." In The Black Power Revolt, ed. by Floyd B. Barber. Boston: Porter,
Sargent, 1968.

Stokes, Gail A. "Black Woman to Black Man." In The Black
Family, ed. by Robert Staples.

Van Ellison, Candice. "History of Harlem." In Harlem on
My Mind: Cultural Capital of Black America 1900-1968,
ed. by Allon Schoener. New York: Random House,
1968.

Walker (Alexander), Margaret. "Religion, Poetry, and History: Foundations for a New Educational System." In
Viewpoints from Black America, ed. by Gladys J. Curry. Englewood Cliffs, N. J. : Prentice-Hall, 1970.

Williams, Kenny J. In the City of Men: Another Story of
Chicago. New York: Townsend Press, 1974.

Williams, Ruby Ora. "In '68 Human Rights Come First,"
The Camp Fire Girl 47 (May, 1968), 3, 4.

_____. "Universal Kinship," The Camp Fire Girl 46
(February, 1967), 3.

Wolfe, Deborah Partridge. "A Faculty Member Responds."
In The Campus and the Racial Crisis, ed. by David

Nichols and Olive Mills.   Washington, D. C. :   American
Council on Education, 1970.

Woods, Gwendolyn Patton.   "Pro-Black, Not Anti-White. "   In
The Campus and the Racial Crisis, ed. by David Nichols
and Olive Mills.   Washington, D. C. :   American Council
on Education, 1970.

Young, Margaret B.   How to Bring Up Your Child without
Prejudice.   Public Affairs Pamphlet No. 373.   New
York.

Young, Pauline A.   "The Negro in Delaware, Past and Present. "   In Delaware, A History of the First State,
Vol. II, ed. by H. Clay Reed.   New York: Lewis Publishing Co. , 1947.

15. FEMINIST ISSUES

Beale, Frances M. "Double Jeopardy: To Be Black and Female." In Sisterhood Is Powerful, ed. by Robin Morgan. New York: Random House (Vintage), 1970.

Black Women's Liberation Group. "State on Birth Control." In Sisterhood Is Powerful, ed. by Robin Morgan. New York: Random House (Vintage), 1970.

Bond, Jean Carey and Pat Perry. "The Changing Role of the Black Woman." In The Black Family: Essays and Studies, ed. by Robert Staples. Belmont, Calif.: Wadsworth Publishers, 1971.

Chisholm, Shirley. "Race, Revolution and Women," Black Scholar 3 (December, 1971), 17-21.

_____. "Racism and Anti-Feminism," Black Scholar 1 (January-February, 1970), 40-43.

_____. Unbought and Unbossed. New York: Avon, 1970.

Cleaver, Kathleen. "Black Scholar Interview," Black Scholar 3 (December, 1971), 54-59.

Conley, Madelyn. "Do Black Women Need the Women's Lib?" Essence 1 (August, 1970), 29-34.

Cummings, Gwenna. "Black Women Often Discussed but Never Understood." In The Black Power Revolt, ed. by Floyd Barbour. Boston: Porter Sargent, 1968.

Davis, Angela. "Racism and Contemporary Literature on Rape," Freedomways 16 (First Quarter, 1976), 25-33. (Specific review of Susan Brownmiller's Against Our Will.)

Dunbar-Nelson, Alice Ruth (Moore).   "Negro Women in War
    Work. " In Scott's Official History of the American Ne-
    gro in the World War, by Emmett J. Scott.   n. p. : 1919.

_____. "Some of the Work of the National Association of
    Colored Women," Long Island Review 7:9 (November,
    1899), 338-339.

Guzman, Jessie Parkhurst.   "The Role of the Black Mammy
    in the Plantation Household," Journal of Negro History
    23 (July, 1938), 349-369.

_____. "The Social Contributions of the Negro Woman
    Since 1940," Negro History Bulletin 11 (January, 1948),
    86-94.

Hunter, Charlayne.   "Black Women and the Liberation Move-
    ment," Black Politician 2 (January, 1971), 15, 39.

Jackson, Jacqueline J.   "Black Man/Black Woman--Creative
    Equals," Essence (November, 1973), 56, 57, 72+ .

_____. "The Plight of Older Black Women in the United
    States," Black Scholar 7:7 (April, 1976), 47-55.

Jackson, Yvonne.   "The Black Female and the Women's Lib-
    eration Movement," Black America 2:1 (March-April,
    1971), 36-37, 63.

Johnson, Willa D. and Thomas L. Green, eds.   Perspectives
    on Afro-American Women.   Washington, D. C. :   ECCA
    Publications, n. d.

Jones, Claudia.   An End to the Neglect of the Problems of
    the Negro Woman.   New York: National Women's Com-
    mission, 1949.

Jones, Viola Julia.   "Women's Liberation as Seen from a
    Black Woman's Point of View," Core 1 (November,
    1970), 16.

Kennedy, Florynce.   "Institutionalized Oppression versus the
    Female. " In Sisterhood Is Powerful, ed. by Robin Mor-
    gan.   New York: Random House (Vintage), 1970.

Koontz, Elizabeth.   "Women of a Minority. " In Voices of

The New Feminism, ed. by Mary Lou Thompson. Boston: Beacon Press, 1971.

Ladner, Joyce. "Tanzanian Women and Nation Building," Black Scholar 3 (December, 1971), 22-28.

_____. Tomorrow's Tomorrow: The Black Woman. New York: Doubleday, 1971.

McDougald, Elsie Johnson. "The Task of Negro Womanhood." In The New Negro, ed. by Alain Locke. New York: Johnson Reprint Corp., 1968.

McGee, Lillian R. "One Not Hung Up on Woman's Liberation Movement," Core 1 (November, 1970), 13.

McKenzie, Marjorie. Fifty Years of Progress for Negro Women. Pittsburgh: Pittsburgh Courier, 1960.

Mossell, Mrs. Gertrude E. The Work of the Afro-American Woman. Philadelphia: C. S. Ferguson Co., 1908 (ca. 1894).

"Mrs. Dunbar Made Strong Argument for Equal Suffrage." Untitled newspaper. AD Papers, Ohio Historical Society, (Roll 7, Frame 1187).

"Mrs. Dunbar on Woman's Suffrage," Harrisburg Telegraph, October 27, 1915. AD Papers, Ohio Historical Society, (Roll 7, Frame 1185).

"Mrs. Dunbar, Suffrage Lecturer," Untitled newspaper. AD Papers, Ohio Historical Society, (Roll 7, Frame 1185).

Newman, Pamela. "Take a Good Look at Your Problems." In Black Women's Liberation, ed. by Maxine Williams and others. New York: Pathfinder Press, 1971.

Reid, Inez Smith. "Together," Black Women. New York: Emerson Hall, 1972.

Rhodes, Barbara. "The Changing Role of the Black Woman." In The Black Family, ed. by Robert Staples. Belmont, Calif.: Wadsworth Press, 1971.

Strong, Augusta. "Negro Women in Freedom's Battles," Freedomways 7 (Fall, 1967), 302-315.

Taylor, Josephine.   "Liberate Ourselves First,"   Core 1:9
    (November, 1970).

Williams, Maxine.   "Why Women's Liberation Is Important
    to Black Women."   In Black Women's Liberation, ed.
    by Maxine Williams and others.   New York: Pathfinder
    Press, 1971.

Willingham, Sandra.   "Our Latest Enemy: Women's Lib,"
    Core 1:9 (November, 1970).

16. OTHER ARTS

a) Illustrators, Painters, Sculptors

Bennett, Gwendolyn. "Winter Landscape," 1936. In The Negro in Art, ed. by Alain Locke. Arlington Heights, Ill. : Metro Books, 1969 (repr. of 1940 ed.)

Blocker, Melonee. "Constant Battle." In An Exhibition of Black Women Artists, May 5-17, 1975. Catalogue. University of California, Santa Barbara.

_____. "Untitled." Oil on canvas. Brockman Gallery, 4334 Degnan Boulevard, Los Angeles, Calif.

Bohanon, Gloria. "Peace and the Child," "Mother Image." In An Exhibition of Black Women Artists, May 5-17, 1975. Catalogue, University of California, Santa Barbara.

Bolton, Shirley. "Opus I," "Black Man." In Black Artists on Art, ed. by Samella Lewis and Ruth C. Waddy. Pasadena, Calif. : Ward Ritchie, n. d. Vol. 2, pp. 44-5.

Brown, Vivian. "Seven Deadly Sins," "Peopled Mountains," "Getting Out." In Black Artists on Art, ed. by Samella Lewis and Ruth C. Waddy. Pasadena, Calif. : Ward Ritchie, n. d.

Burke, Selma. "Lafayette." In Modern Negro Art, ed. by James Amos Porter. New York: Arno Press, 1969 (reprint of 1943 ed.).

Burroughs, Margaret. "Sojourner Truth." In American Negro Art, ed. by Cedric Dove. Boston: New York Graphic Society, 1965. p. 20.

96

Art Works in This Section

1. Papier-maché mask by Beulah Woodard, part of a one-person show at Los Angeles County Museum, 1937. Photo by Mirriam Matthews.
2. Bronze bust of Sir Perry M. Smith. Last piece of sculpture by Beulah Woodard before her death in 1955. Photo by Mirriam Matthews.
3. "Which Way?" by Elizabeth Catlett.
4. Sterling silver raised bowl with purple heart and silver plated steel turned base, by Evangeline J. Montgomery. Completed, 1973. Photo by J. P. Eubanks.
5. "Black Women," by Barbara Dumetz.
6. "Tub, Saturday Night," by Varnette Honeywood.
7. Beulah Woodard, sculptor, with some of her works. Collection of Mirriam Matthews.
8. "Sunday Morning, Friendship Baptist Church," by Lizzetta LeFalle.
9. Detail: "Plant Life," by Gloria Simmons.

SIR PERRY M. SMITH
INTERNATIONAL CHIEF GRAND MENTOR
OF THE KNIGHTS AND DAUGHTERS
OF TABOR

Butler, Sheryle. "Composition." In Black Artists on Art,
ed. by Samella Lewis and Ruth C. Waddy. Pasadena,
Calif. : Ward Ritchie, n. d. Vol. 2, p. 31.

Catlett, Elizabeth. "El Baile," and "Which Way?" In An
Exhibition of Black Women Artists. Catalogue, University of California, Santa Barbara.

_____. Figura. Sol Lieber Collection, New York.

_____. Negro Girl, marble, 1939. In The Negro in Art,
ed. by Alain Locke. Arlington Heights, Ill. : Metro
Books, 1969. p. 115.

_____. Negro Mother and Child, bronze, 1940, Alonzo K.
Aden.

_____. Negro Woman, wood. Atlanta University.

Chase, Barbara. Adam and Eve, bronze, 1958; "Bulls,"
1958. At: Galleria L'Oblisco, Rome.

_____. Victorious Bullfighter, bronze, 1958. Dr. Perry
Ottenburg, Pa.

Conwill, Kinshasha. "Untitled." Mixed media. Brockman
Gallery, 4334 Degnan Boulevard, Los Angeles, Calif.

Cremer, Marva. "Strange Journey," "Do You Know What
I'm Doing?" Lithographs. In Black Artists on Art,
ed. by Samella Lewis and Ruth C. Waddy. Pasadena,
Calif. : Ward Ritchie, n. d. Vol. 1, Rev. ed., p. 94.

Dumetz, Barbara. "Black Woman." In An Exhibition of Black
Women Artists. Catalogue, University, Santa Barbara.

Egozi, Mikele. "The Story Teller." In An Exhibition of Black
Women Artists. Catalogue, University of California,
Santa Barbara.

Fakeye, Brenda. "The Curse of Noah." In An Exhibition of
Black Women Artists. Catalogue, University of California, Santa Barbara.

Farrell, Duneen. "Fertility." In An Exhibition of Black Women Artists. Catalogue, University of California, Santa
Barbara.

Alice T. Gafford at age 80.   She began art work at 49,
and was 91 on August 15, 1977.   Photo by Mirriam Matthews

Fletcher, Mikele Egozi. "The Black Madonna." In Black
Artists on Art, ed. by Samella Lewis and Ruth C. Waddy. Pasadena, Calif. : Ward Ritchie, n. d.

Fuller, Meta Warick. Ethiopia Awakening. Schomburg Library, New York.

_____. Water Boy. Harmon Foundation.

Gafford, Alice T. "Champagne Break," oil. Permanent collection of the Howard University Art Gallery, Washington, D. C.

_____. "Still Life with Antiques." Permanent collection,
Charles Bowers Memorial Museum, Santa Ana, Calif.

_____. "Tea Party," oil. Permanent collection, Long
Beach Museum of Art, Long Beach, Calif.

Hildebrand, Camille. Psalm 1 and Urn. In the collection
of the artist, Long Beach, California.

Honeywood, Varnette. "African Woman," acrylic on canvas.
Brockman Gallery, 4334 Degnan Boulevard, Los Angeles,
Calif.

_____. "Birthday," "#3, Tub Saturday Night." In An Ex-
hibition of Black Women Artists. Catalogue, University
of California, Santa Barbara.

Humphrey, Margo. "Zebra Series," lithograph. In Black
Artists on Art, ed. by Samella Lewis and Ruth C. Waddy. Pasadena, Calif. : Ward Ritchie, n. d. Vol. 1,
rev. ed. , p. 9.

Jeffries, Rosalind. "Maska," "Masks." In An Exhibition of
Black Women Artists. Catalogue, University of California, Santa Barbara.

Johnson, Karen. Illustrator, Poems Around Struggle and
Love by Mshariri S. Weusi. San Francisco: Julian
Richardson Associates, 1976.

_____. Untitled poster of African boys. Available, San
Francisco: Marcus Bookstore.

Jones, Lois Mailou. "Dance Mask," mixed media, 22 1/4 x

35 1/2, 1972; "Moon Masque," acrylic-collage, 41" x
29". In Black Artists on Art, ed. by Samella Lewis
and Ruth C. Waddy. Pasadena, Calif. : Ward Ritchie,
n. d. Vol. 1, rev. ed. , pp. 97-98.

LeFalle, Lizzetta. "Sunday Morning, Friendship Baptist
Church. " "Sunday Morning, Newspapers. " "Red Hots. "
In An Exhibition of Black Women Artists, May 5-17,
1975. Santa Barbara: University of California.

Lewis, Edmonia. Abraham Lincoln, marble; Asleep. In
Modern Negro Art, ed. by James Amos Porter. New
York: Arno Press, 1969.

_____. Hagar, marble. Frederick Douglass Institute.

_____. James Peck Thomas, marble, 1880. Mrs. James
Blair.

_____. Old Indian Arrow Maker and His Daughter, mar-
ble, 1872. James H. Ricau, Piermont, New York.

Lewis, Samella. "20th Century Nefertiti," "Colonial Scene,"
and "Migrants. " In An Exhibition of Black Women
Artists. Santa Barbara: University of California.

McClinton, Diane T. "Lost in the City," acrylic on canvas.
Brockman Gallery, 4334 Degnan Boulevard, Los Angeles, Calif.

Marshall, Enrica. "Energy Out," collage. Brockman Gallery, 4334 Degnan Boulevard, Los Angeles, Calif.

Montgomery, E(vangeline). J. "Black Jade Ancestral Box. "
Sterling silver cast ancestral box, 1973, 2"x2; 2x2".
Collection of the artist, San Francisco Art Commissioner.

_____. "Silver Bowl. " Sterling silver raised bowl with
purple heart and silver-plated steel turned base, 1973.
6". Collection of the artist, San Francisco Art Commissioner.

Okwumabua, Constance. "Epilogwu Dancers," acrylic, 5'x6'.
In Black Artists on Art, ed. by Samella Lewis and
Ruth C. Waddy. Pasadena, Calif. : Ward Ritchie, n. d.
Vol. 1, rev. ed. , p. 115.

Pecot, Monica D. "Untitled," and "T. Sphere World." In
An Exhibition of Black Women Artists. Santa Barbara:
University of California.

Perkins, Angela. "From Reflections to Reality," acrylic on
canvas. Brockman Gallery, 4334 Degnan Boulevard,
Los Angeles, Calif.

Rogers, Brenda. "Flower Pot." 16"x20". In Black Artists
on Art, ed. by Samella Lewis and Ruth C. Waddy, Pasadena, Calif. : Ward Ritchie, n. d. Vol. 1, rev. ed. ,
p. 63.

Simmons, Donna. "Untitled." In An Exhibition of Black
Women Artists. Santa Barbara: University of California.

Simmons, Gloria Brown. Detail: Plant Life.

_____. "Horizon." In An Exhibition of Black Women
Artists. Santa Barbara: University of California.

_____. Kiss the Sun, Largest Sphere, Rain Lips, 1' dia.

_____. Porcelain Teapot and Warmer, 13".

_____. Untitled ceramic, 20"-22".

Simon, Jewel W. "Walk Together Children," mono-print,
16"x21", 1964. In Black Artists on Art, ed. by Samella Lewis and Ruth C. Waddy. Pasadena, Calif. : Ward
Ritchie, n. d. Vol. 1, rev. ed. , p. 108.

Waddy, Ruth G. "Daisies," oil, 1966. "The Fence," linocut, 1969. "The Key, " linocut, 1969. In Black Artists
on Art, ed. by Samella Lewis and Ruth C. Waddy.
Pasadena, Calif.: Ward Ritchie, n. d. Vol. 1.

Waring, Laura. "Alonso Aden." "Frankie." In Modern Negro Art, ed. by James Amos Porter. New York: Arno
Press, 1969.

Wayner, Carole J. "The Children." In An Exhibition of
Black Women Artists. Santa Barbara: University of
California.

White, Cynthia. "Untitled." In An Exhibition of Black Women Artists. Santa Barbara: University of California.

Woodard, Beulah. Libyan Mother, mahogany. Permanent
collection of Bowers Museum, Santa Ana, Calif.

_____. Masai Warrior, terra cotta, 13", 1937; Golden
State Mutual Life Insurance Company, Los Angeles,
Calif.

_____. Maudelle, terra cotta, 13", 1939; collection of
Mirriam Matthews, Los Angeles, Calif.

_____. Travail. Korean mother and daughter, camphor
wood, 32"; permanent collection, Los Angeles City Art
Department.

b) Music: Arrangers, Composers and Lyricists

Akers, Doris. "Ask What You Will," "He Knows and He
Cares," "I Cannot Fail the Lord," "Lord Keep My Mind
on Thee," "My Song of Assurance," "Prayer Is the
Answer," "Sweet, Sweet Spirit," "Trouble," "You Can't
Beat God Giving." In: Doris Akers' Favorite Gospel
Songs, Vol. I. Hollywood, Calif.: Manna Music, Inc.,
1328 N. Highland Avenue.

Armstead, Josie, Valerie Simpson, and Nickolas Ashford.
"I Don't Need No Doctor." Hollywood, Calif.: Baby
Monica Music Inc.; New York: Renleigh Music Corp.

Armstrong, Lillian Hardin (Lillian Hardin). "Dropping
Schucks." Music Corp. of America, 1926.

_____. "Flat Foot." MCA, 1926.

_____. "I'm Gonna Get Cha." MCA, 1926.

_____. "Jazz Lips." MCA, 1926.

_____. "King of the Zuluz." MCA, 1926.

_____. "Papa Dip." MCA, 1926.

_____. "Perdido Street Blues." MCA, 1926.

_____. "Skit-Dat-De Dat." MCA, 1926.

_____. "Tight Blues." MCA, 1926.

_____. "You're Next." MCA, 1926.

_____, and Walter Melrose. "My Sweet Lovin' Man."
New York: Melrose Music Corp., 1923.

Ashby, Dorothy. "A-Wandering." In Afro-America Sings,
ed. by Ollie McFarland and others. Detroit: Board of
Education, 1971.

Austin, Lovie. "I've Got the Blues for Rampart Street."
New York: Mills Music Corp., 1923.

Ayo, Zena. "Bring Peace to the World." Vocal. Hollywood: Zayo Publications, 1960.

_____. "Save Me." Hollywood: Zayo, 1962.

Baker, Josephine and Spencer Williams. "Black Bottom
Fall." MCA, 1927.

_____. "Lonesome Lovesick Blues." MCA, 1926.

Bonds, Margaret. The Ballad of the Brown King. Text by
Langston Hughes. New York: Sam Fox Publ. Co.,
1961. A Christmas cantata for chorus of mixed voices
(SATB) with piano accompaniment. Score, 56 pp.

_____. The Ballad of the Brown King. "Mary had a Lit-
tle Baby." New York: Sam Fox 1962 (piano); 1963
(women's chorus)

_____. "Bright Star." Beverly Hills, Calif.: Pasca.
(vocal)

_____. "Children's Sleep." Words by Vernon Glasser.
New York: Carl Fischer.

_____. "Didn't It Rain." New York: Beekman Music,
1967; Bryn Mawr, Pa.: Theodore Presser, 1900. (for
medium voice)

_____. "Dream Variation." Words by Langston Hughes.
New York: Recordi, 1959.

_____. "Dry Bones." New York: G. Schirmer.

_____. "Dry Bones," "I'll Reach Heaven," "Lord, I Just
Can't Keep from Crying," "Sit Down Servant," "You Can
Tell the World." In Five Spirituals. New York: Mu-
tual Music Society.

_____. "Ezek'l Saw the Wheel." New York: Beckman
Music Co., 1959.

_____. "Georgia." With Andy Razaff and Joe Davis. New
York: Dorsey Brothers.

_____. "Go Tell It on the Mountain." New York: Beekman
Music Co., 1962.

_____. He's Got the Whole World in His Hands. New
York: Beekman Music Co. (songs with piano)

_____. Hold On. New York: Mercury, 1962; New York:
G. Schirmer. (Arr. songs with piano)

_____. "I Got a Home in-a That Rock." New York:
Beekman Music Co., 1959. (Arr.)

_____. "I Shall Pass Through This World." London:
Bourne Co., 1966.

_____. "I Too." Words by Langston Hughes. New York:
Ricordi, 1959.

_____. "Joshua Fit Da Battle of Jericho." New York:
Beekman Music Co., 1967.

_____. "Minstrel Man." Words by Langston Hughes.
New York: Ricordi, 1959.

_____. "The Negro Speaks of Rivers." Lyrics by Lang-
ston Hughes. New York: Handy Brothers, 1946.

_____. The Nile Fantasy. Written by Philippa Duke Schuy-
ler. Premiered in America, Town Hall, New York,
September 24, 1967.

_____. "Peach Tree Street." With Andy Razaff and Joe
Davis. New York: Dorsey Brothers, 1939.

_____. "Rainbow Gold." Words by Roger Chaney. New
York: Chappell and Co., 1956.

_____. "Sing A-Ho That I Had the Wings of a Dove."
New York: Chappell, 1960.

_____. "Sinner, Please Don't Let This Harvest Pass."
1960.

_____. "Spring Will Be So Sad." New York: Mutual
Music Society, 1941.

_____. Three Dream Portraits. Words by Langston
Hughes. Poems from The Dream Keeper. New York:
Ricordi, 1959. (for voice and piano)

_____. "Three Sheeps in a Pasture." New York: Clar-
ence Williams, 1940.

_____. "To a Brown Girl Dead." Words by Countee
Cullen. Boston: R. D. Row Music Company; New York:
G. Schirmer.

_____. "Troubled Water." New York: Sam Fox, 1967.

_____. "When the Dove Enters In." With Langston
Hughes. 1963.

_____. "You Can Tell the World." For mixed chorus
(SATB). Arr. Charles N. Smith. New York: Mutual
Music Society. Score, 8 pp. (MCS, 123.)

Brown, Elaine. "And All Stood By," "The End of Silence,"
"The Panther," "Very Black Man." In Seize the Time.
Vault, Stereo 131.

Caesar, Shirley. "I'll Go." Shirley Caesar and the Institu-
tional Choir of Brooklyn. HOB 266.

_____. "Stranger on the Road." Shirley Caesar and the
Caesar Singers. HOB 299.

Carlisle, Una Mae. "Walkin' by the River." Gower Music
Company, Inc.

Cleaver, Esther A. "Can You See God?" Los Angeles:
Dex-es Publishing House; Newark, N.J.: Savoy Music
Co., 1974.

Coltrane, Alice. "The Anka of Amen-ka," "Battle at

Armageddon, " "Hare Krishna, " "Oh Allah, " "Sit a Ram. "
Universal Consciousness.   Impulse AS 9210.

_____. "Atmic Peace," "Gospel Trane," "I Want to See
You," "Lovely Sky Boat," "Ohnedruth," "Organic Be-
loved. " A Monastic Trio.   ABC Records, Inc. ,
AS 9156.

_____. "Isis and Osiris," "Journey in Satchidnanda,"
"Shiva-Loka," "Something about John Coltrane," "Stop
Over Bombay. " Journey in Satchidnanda.   Impulse
Stereo AS 9203.

Cox, Ida.   "Bone Orchard Blues. " Northern Music Corp. ,
1928.

_____. " 'Fore Day Creep. " Northern Music Corp. , 1928.

_____. "Graveyard Dream Blues. " Northern Music Corp.,
1923.

_____. "Midnight Hour Blues. " Northern Music Corp. ,
1928.

_____. "Western Union Blues. " Northern Music Corp. ,
1928.

_____, and Lovie Austin.   "Weary Way Blues. " Northern
Music Corp. , 1924.

_____, and Jesse Crump.   "Death Letter Blues. " North-
ern Music Corp. , 1924.

Douroux, Margaret Pleasant.   "An Instrument for Thee. "
Los Angeles: Rev. Earl A. Pleasant Publishing, 5116
Veronica Street, 1975.

_____. "Deep Water. " Los Angeles: Reverend Earl
Pleasant Publ. Co. (4269 S. Figueroa St. , 90037) 1975.

_____. "Give Me a Clean Heart. " Los Angeles: Rev-
erend Earl Pleasant Publ. Co. , [n. d.].

_____. "God Is Not Dead. " Los Angeles: Reverend Earl
Pleasant Publ. Co. , 1973.

_____. "God Is Passing Out Blessings. " Los Angeles:
Reverend Earl Pleasant Publ. Co. , [n. d.].

_____. "God Made a Man." Los Angeles: Reverend
Earl Pleasant Publ. Co., 1975.

_____. "I'm Glad." Los Angeles: Reverend Earl Plea-
sant Publ. Co., (Sacred song), [n. d.].

_____. "I'm Gonna Take My Burdens." Los Angeles:
Reverend Earl Pleasant Publ. Co., [n. d.].

_____. "The Lord Is Speaking." Los Angeles: Reverend
Earl Pleasant Publ. Co., [n. d.].

_____. "The Lord Lifted Me." Los Angeles: Reverend
Earl Pleasant Publ. Co., 1975.

_____. "Love Song." Los Angeles: Reverend Earl Plea-
sant Publ. Co., 1975.

_____. "My Help Cometh from the Lord." Los Angeles:
Reverend Earl Pleasant Publ. Co., [n. d.].

_____. "Only God." Los Angeles: Reverend Earl Plea-
sant Publ. Co., 1974.

_____. "Show Me the Way." Los Angeles: Reverend
Earl Pleasant Publ. Co., 1973.

_____. "Strengthen Me." Los Angeles: Reverend Earl
Pleasant Publ. Co., 1974.

_____. "Teach Me How to Love." As recorded by Mount
Moriah Baptist Church, 470 West 43rd Street, Los Angeles, Calif. Los Angeles: Jina Music Co.

_____. "There Is God." Los Angeles: Reverend Earl
Pleasant Publ. Co., 1973.

_____. "We're Blest." Los Angeles: Reverend Earl
Pleasant Publ. Co., [n. d.].

_____. "What Have You Done for Jesus?" Los Angeles:
Reverend Earl Pleasant Publ. Co., [n. d.].

_____. "What Shall I Render." Los Angeles: Reverend
Earl Pleasant Publ. Co., 1975.

DuBois, Shirley Graham. Tom-Tom. Three-act opera, premiered in concert form by NBC Radio, June 26, 1932;

stage performance, Cleveland Stadium, 1932.

Evanti, Lillian. "Dedication." Words by Georgia Douglas
Johnson. New York: Handy Brothers, 1948.

————. "Forward March to Victory." 1943. (Inspired
during the Battle of the Coral Sea--completed after victory in Africa and Capitulation of Pantelleria and Pam-
pedusa.) Translated into Chinese, Dutch, Spanish,
Czechoslovak, French, Yugoslav.

————. "Hail to Fair Washington." Words by Georgia D.
Johnson. 1953.

————. "High Flight." Words by John Gillespie Magee,
Jr. New York: Handy Bros., 1948.

————. "Himno Panamericano." Arranged by Felix Guen-
ther (for three-part treble, 1st soprano, 2nd soprano
and alto). New York: Edward B. Marks Music Corp.,
RCA Building, 1941.

————. "I'm Yours for Tonight." New York: Columbia
Music Co., [n.d.].

————. "The Mighty Rapture." Words by Edwin Markham.
New York: Handy Bros., 1948.

————. "My Little Prayer." Words by Mrs. Bruce
Evans. New York: Handy Bros., 1948.

————. "Speak to Him Thou." Words by Alfred Tennyson.
New York: Handy Bros., 1948.

————. "Thank You Again and Again." New York: Handy
Bros., 1948.

————. "Tomorrow's World." Words by Georgia Douglas
Johnson, 1948. (Chorus, SATB)

————. "Twenty-Third Psalm." New York: Handy Bros.,
1947.

————. "United Nations." 1953. (for mixed voices)

Fitzgerald, Ella and Al Freeman. "A-Tisket A-Tasket."
New York: Robbins Music Corp., 1937.

_____, and Kenneth Watts. "Oh, But I Do." New York:
Leeds Music Corp., 1945.

Franklin, Aretha. "All the King's Horses." Copyright A.
Franklin, 1972. c/o Feinman and Krasilovsky.

_____. "Call Me." Aretha's Greatest Hits. Atlantic,
SD 8295.

Grant, Coot (Liola Wilson), and Socks Wilson. "Do Your
Duty," "Down in the Dumps," "Gimma a Pigfoot," "Take
Me for a Buggy Ride." Recorded by Bessie Smith,
Bessie Smith: The World's Greatest Blues Singer. Co-
lumbia, GP 33.

Grant, Micki (Minnie McCutcheon). "All I Need," "Billie
Holiday," "Children's Rhymes," "Do a Little Living for
Peace," "Don't Bother Me, I Can't Cope," "Good Vibra-
tions," "Harlem Streets," "Help," "I Gotta Keep Movin',"
"It Takes a Whole Lot of Human Feeling," "Lock Up the
Doors," "My Love's So Good," "My Name Is Man,"
"They Keep Coming," "Time Brings About a Change,"
"You Think I Got Rhythm," and others. In Don't Bother
Me, I Can't Cope. Performed at the Edison Theatre,
New York, and at the Mark Taper, Los Angeles, 1972.
Tommy Valando, publisher.

_____. "Behind a Moonbeam." Hastings Music Corp.,
[n. d.].

_____. "Come Back, Baby." Copyright, Micki Grant.

_____. "Perfect If." Copyright, Micki Grant.

Green, Lil. "In the Dark" (or, "Romance in the Dark").
Duchen Music Corp.

Hackley, Emma Azalea (Smith). "Carola." New York: Handy Bros., 1953.

Hagan, Helen. Concerto in C Minor. Unpublished. Played
by Ms. Hagan at her graduation from the Yale University School of Music, 1911, with New Haven Symphony
Orchestra. (for piano and orchestra)

Handy, D. Antoinette. Hommage a Haute Savoie. Ettrick,
Va.: BM & M, P.O. Box 103.

Harris, Margaret R. "Collage One." 1970. 17 pp.

_____. "Dear Love." 1970.

_____. "Grievin'." 1970. 4 pp.

_____. "Tonite's Goodbye." 1970.

Hegamin, Lucille. "Mississippi Blues." MCA.

Hill, Bertha. "Chippie," "Pratt's City Blues." MCA, 1926.

Holiday, Billie. "Billie's Blues" (or, "I Love My Man").
New York: Edward Marks, 1962. (for voice and piano,
pl. no. 14603)

_____. "Fine and Mellow." Edwards Marks, 1940.

_____, and Arthur Herzog. "Don't Explain." Northern
Music Corp.; also Matrix, No. 73006A.

_____. "God Bless the Child." Edward Marks, 1969.
(vocal duet with piano, pl. no. 15408)

RECORDINGS OF BILLIE HOLIDAY:

All or Nothing at All. Verve, 68329.

The Best of Billie Holiday. Verve, V68808.

Billie Holiday: God Bless the Child. 2 records. Columbia, G30782.

Billie Holiday: The Golden Years, Vol. 1. Columbia,
C3L-21.

Billie Holiday: The Golden Years, Vol. 2. Columbia,
C3L-40.

Billie Holiday's Greatest Hits. Columbia, Monaural
CL2666.

Billie Holiday's Greatest Hits. Phonodisc. Decca,
DL 75040. Microgroove and Stereophonic.

Ella Fitzgerald and Billie Holiday at Newport. American Record Society, 1937.

Essential Billie Holiday. Verve, stereo 68410; eight-
track cartridge 8140; monaural 8410.

Gallant Lady. Monmouth-Evergreen Records, MES 7046.

Lady Day: A Collection of Classic Jazz Interpretations
by Billie Holiday. All-star accompaniments. Columbia, CL 637.

Lady in Satin, Billie Holiday. Columbia, CL 1157;
Stereo CS 8040.

Lady Love. United Artists, 15014.

Lady Love. United Artists, stereo 5636.

Lady Love. Solid State, stereo 18040.

The Lady Sings, Vol. 1. Ace of Hearts, monaural 151.

"Lover Man." The Birth of Soul! Decca Records,
DL 7925. (Louis Armstrong, Ella Fitzgerald, Billie
Holiday, Sister Rosetta Tharpe, Louis Jordan, Buddy
Johnson, Lionel Hampton, Ray-O-Vacs, The Flamingos,
Jay McShann, Lucky Millinder.) Stereo.

Solitude. Verve, stereo 68074; eight-track cartridge
8140; monaural 8074.

Hunter, Alberta. "Down Hearted Blues." Music by Lovie
Austin. New York: Mills Music Corp., 1923.

_____. "I Got a Mind to Ramble." New York: Leeds.

_____. "I Want to Thank You, Lord," New York: Leeds.

_____. "The Love I Have for You." Peer International.

_____. "Streets Paved with Gold." New York: Fred
Fischer Co., Inc.

_____. "Will the Day Ever Come When I Can Rest."
New York: Fred Fischer.

_____. "You Better Change." Handy Bros.

_____, Ethel Waters, and Fletcher Henderson. "Down
South Blues." Mills.

Jenkins, Ella. The Ella Jenkins Song Book for Children.
Illustrator, Peggy Lipschitz. New York: Oak Publications, 1973.

Jessye, Eva. My Spirituals. Illustrated by Millar of the
Roland Company; ed. by Gordon Whyte and Hugo Frey.
New York: Robbins-Engel, Inc. , 1927.

Eva Jessye.   Photo by Bob Kalmbach

_____. "Nobody. " New York: Marks, 1956.   (for four-
part men's chorus and piano, pl. no. 13419)

_____. Paradise Lost and Regained.   Folk-Oratorio.
John Milton, librettist.   Performed at Glassboro State
College, Glassboro, N. J. , May 5, 1974.

_____. "Simon, The Fisherman" (A Negro Song).   Bos-
ton: Birchard and Co.   (for chorus of mixed voices
with narrators)   Arr.   Eva Jessye.

_____. "When the Saints Go Marching In. " New York:
Marks, 1956.   (for chorus and piano, Eva Jessye Choral
Series, pl. no. 13416)

Johnson, Edith. "Nickel's Worth of Liver." Northern Music
    Corp. , 1929.

King, Betty Jackson. "Dawn." Poem by Paul Laurence Dun-
    bar. (for voice)

_____. "Fantastic Mirror." (for piano)

_____. Four Season Sketches: "Spring Intermezzo,"
    "Summer Interlude," "Autumn Dance," "Winter Holiday."
    (for piano)

_____. "God Shall Wipe Away All Tears." (requiem for
    voice)

_____. "A Lover's Plea." Poem by Shakespeare. (for
    voice)

_____. "Mother Goose Parade." (for piano)

_____. Nuptial Suite: "Processional," "Nuptial Song,"
    "Recessional." (for organ)

_____. Saul of Tarsus (Biblical opera). Excerpts of this
    and the other works listed above were performed by The
    Imperial Opera Company, Chicago, Ill. , at the River-
    side Church, New York, August 12, 1972. Saul of Tar-
    sus was premiered at DuSable High School, Chicago,
    1952. The Biblical libretto was compiled by the late
    Reverend Fred D. Jackson.

Liston, Melba Doretta. "Blues Melba," "You Don't Say."
    Melba Liston and Her 'Bones. ' MGM Stereo Se 1013.

Lutcher, Nellie. "He's a Real Gone Guy." Criterion Music
    Corp.

_____. "Hurry On Down." Criterion Music Corp.

McCanns, Shirley Graham (DuBois). "I Promise." Words
    by Lorenz Graham. New York: Handy Bros, 1934.

McFarland, Ollie. "Alphabet Travelogue." In Afro-America
    Sings, ed. by Ollie McFarland and others. Detroit:
    Board of Education, 1971.

_____. "Balloons" (Lullaby). In Afro-America Sings, ed.
    by Ollie McFarland and others. Detroit: Board of Educa-
    tion, 1971.

Betty Jackson King.   Photo by Cleodia H. Lyles

_____. "Fireworks." In Afro-America Sings, ed. by Ollie McFarland and others. Detroit: Board of Education, 1971.

_____, arranger. "O Mary." In Afro-America Sings, ed. by Ollie McFarland and others. Detroit: Board of Education, 1971.

_____. "Rise Up Shepherd and Follow." In Afro-America Sings, ed. by Ollie McFarland and others. Detroit: Board of Education, 1971.

McLin, Lena J. "All the Earth Sing Unto the Lord." Text based on Psalm 96. Park Ridge, Ill.: Neil A. Kjos, 1967. (SATB a capella. Ed. 5459)

_____. "The Colors of the Rainbow." New York: Pro Arte, 1971. (mixed chorus)

_____. Eucharest of the Soul: A Liturgical Mass. Park Ridge, Ill.: GWMC, 1972. (SATB accompanied. Ed. GC 41)

_____. "For the Air That's Pure." Park Ridge, Ill.: General Words and Music Co., 1970.

_____. Free at Last! A Portrait of Martin Luther King, Jr. Park Ridge, Ill.: Neil A Kjos, 1973. (SATB chorus, Soprano, and Baritone [or mezzo-soprano] Solo)

_____. "Friendship." Park Ridge, Ill.: General Words and Music Co., 1972 (SATB accompanied. Ed. GC 39)

_____. "Gwendolyn Brooks." Park Ridge, Ill.: General Words and Music Co., 1972. (SATB accompanied. ED. GC 21)

_____. "I Love No One But." In In This World, pp. 28-33.

_____. "If They Ask You Why He Came." Park Ridge, Ill.: General Words and Music Co., 1971. Ed. GC 35.

_____. In This World. Park Ridge, Ill.: General Words and Music Co., and Neil A. Kjos. (SATB)

_____. "The Little Baby." Park Ridge, Ill.: Neil A. Kjos, 1971. (SATB accompanied with optional solo. Ed. 5855)

_____. "Memory." Poem by Paul L. Dunbar. Park
Ridge, Ill. : General Words and Music Co. , 1976.
(SATB with optional accompaniment. Ed. GC 79)

_____. "Miracles for Me." In In This World, pp. 21-27.

_____. "New Born King." Park Ridge, Ill. : General
Words and Music Co. , 1972. (SATB, a cappella; piano
for rehearsal only. Ed. Gc 23)

_____. "People Talk." In In This World, pp. 34-37.

_____. "Psalm 100." Westbury, N. Y. : Pro Arte, 1971.
(mixed chorus)

_____. "Psalm 117." Westbury, N. Y. : Pro Arte, 1971.

_____. "Sanctus and Benedictus." Park Ridge, Ill. :
General Words and Music Co. , 1971. (SATB accompanied)

_____. "Since He Came Into My Life." Park Ridge, Ill. :
Neil A. Kjos and General Words and Music Co. , 1976.
(SATB accompanied. Ed. GC 80)

_____. "Te Deum Laudamus." Park Ridge, Ill. : Gener-
al Words and Music Co. , 1976. (SATB accompanied.
Ed. Gc 56)

_____. "The Torch Has Been Passed." Park Ridge, Ill. :
General Words and Music Co. , 1974. (SATB a cappella.
Ed. GC 20)

_____. "What Will You Put Under Your Christmas Tree?"
Park Ridge, Ill. : General Words and Music Co. , 1971.
(SATB accompanied. Ed. GC 22)

_____. "Winter, Spring, Summer, Autumn." Park Ridge,
Ill. : Neil A. Kjos, 1974. (SATB. ED. 58 99)

_____, arranger. "Cert'nly Lord, Cert'nly Lord." Park
Ridge, Ill. : Neil A. Kjos, 1967. (Ed. 5458)

_____, arranger. "Down by the River." Park Ridge,
Ill. : Neil A. Kjos. (SATB a cappella. Ed. 5915)

_____, arranger. "Glory, Glory Hallelujah." Traditional

Negro Spiritual. Park Ridge, Ill. : Neil A. Kjos, 1966. (Ed. 5430)

_____, arranger. "I'm So Glad Trouble Don't Last Al ways." Park Ridge, Ill. : Neil A. Kjos, 1974. (SATB a cappella. Ed. 5898)

_____, arranger. "My God Is So High. " Park Ridge, Ill. : Neil A. Kjos, 1972. (SATB a cappella. Ed. 5881)

_____, arranger. "Writ'en Down My Name. " Park Ridge, Ill. : Neil A. Kjos, 1967. (SATB a cappella with baritone solo. Ed. 5460)

Moore, Dorothy Rudd. Baroque Suite for Unaccompanied Cello. Three movements. New York: Rudmor.

_____. Dirge and Deliverance. Two movements. New York: Rudmor. (for cello and piano)

_____. Dream and Variations. New York: Rudmor Publishers (33 Riverside Drive). Duration 18 min. Commissioned by Ludwig Olshansky. (for piano)

_____. From the Dark Tower: A Song Cycle for Mezzo-Soprano, Cello, and Piano. A setting of eight poems by Black American poets. New York: Rudmor.

_____. From the Dark Tower. An orchestration of four songs from the song cycle of the same name. (for mezzo-soprano and orchestra) New York: Rudmor.

_____. "Lament for Nine Instruments. " One movement. New York: Rudmor.

_____. Modes for String Quartet. Three movements. New York: Rudmor.

_____. Moods for Viola and Cello. A duo. Three movements. New York: Rudmor.

_____. "Reflections. " One movement. New York: Rudmor. (for symphonic wind ensemble)

_____. Songs. A song cycle. (A setting of twelve quatrains from "The Rubaiyat" of Omar Khayyam.) (for mezzo-soprano and oboe) New York: Rudmor.

Dorothy Rudd Moore

_____. "Symphony No. 1." One movement. New York:
Rudmore.

_____. Three Pieces for Violin and Piano. Three move-
ments. New York: Rudmore.

_____. Trio No. 1. Three movements. New York:
Rudmore. (for violin, cello and piano)

Moore, Undine Smith. "Bound for Canaan's Land." New
York: Witmark Music Publishers, 1960. (mixed chorus)

_____. "Daniel, Daniel Servant of the Lord." New York:
Witmark, 1953. (mixed chorus)

_____. "Fare Ye Well." New York: Witmark, 1951.
(mixed chorus)

_____. "Hail, Warrior." New York: Witmark, 1958.
(mixed chorus)

_____. "Let Us Make Man in Our Own Image." New
York: Witmark, 1960. (mixed chorus)

_____. "Mother to Son." New York: Witmark, 1955.
(mixed chorus)

_____. "Striving After God." New York: Witmark, 1958.
(mixed chorus)

Nickerson, Camille. "Gue-Gue solingaie (Lemoine)." New
York: Leeds, 1948. (for four-part chorus and piano)

_____, arranger and harmonizer. "Dance, Baby, Dance."
In Five Creole Folk Songs. Boston: Boston Music Co.,
1947.

_____. "Dear I Love You So." In Five Creole Folk
Songs. Boston: Boston Music Co., 1947.

_____. "Go to Sleep." In Five Creole Folk Songs. Bos-
ton: Boston Music Co., 1947.

_____. "Lizette, My Dearest One." In Five Creole Folk
Songs. Boston: Boston Music Co., 1947.

_____. "Mister Banjo." In Five Creole Folk Songs. Bos-
ton: Boston Music Co., 1947.

Perry, Julia. "Be Merciful unto Me, O God." Words from Psalm 57:1,2. New York: Galaxy Music Corp., (for chorus of mixed voices, with soprano and bass solos; organ acc. available)

_____. "By the Sea." New York: Galaxy.

_____. "Carillon Heigh Ho," ed. by John Finley Williamson. New York: Carl Fischer. (SATB divided a capella)

_____. The Cask of Amontillado. One-act opera. New York: Southern Music Co.

_____. "Contretemps." (for orchestra)

_____. "Fragments of Letters of Saint Catherine." New York: Southern Music Co. (for solo voice, chorus, and orchestra)

_____. "Frammenti dalle Lettere de Santa Caterina." New York: Southern Music Co. (for soprano, mixed chorus, and orchestra)

_____. "Free At Last." New York: Galaxy. (Arr.)

_____. Homunculus. New York: Carl Fischer, 1966. (for percussion and harp)

_____. "Homunculus." New York: Carl Fischer (for soprano and percussionists)

_____. "How Beautiful Are the Feet." New York: Galaxy, 1964. (medium voice and piano)

_____. Lord! What Shall I Do? Boston: McLaughlin and Reilly Co.

_____. "Our Thanks to Thee." Anthem for Thanksgiving or general use. New York: Galaxy, 1951. (chorus or mixed voices with contralto solo. Piano acc. available)

_____. "Pastoral." New York: Southern Music Co., 1962. (for flute and strings sextet)

_____. "Short Piece." 8 minutes. New York: Southern Music Co.

_____. Simple Symphony, No. 12. Two movements, 1973. (for strings, 3 clarinets, 3 trumpets, percussion. Duration 10 minutes)

_____. "Songs of Our Savior." New York: Galaxy, 1953. (for chorus of mixed voices; unaccompanied)

_____. "Stabat Mater." New York: Southern Music Co. Latin poem by Jacophone da Todi, XIII Century. Translation by the composer. Score in Latin and English words. (for contralto and string quartet or string orchestra)

_____. Ye, Who Seek the Truth. New York: Galaxy. (for chorus of mixed voices with tenor solo; organ acc. also available)

RECORDINGS OF JULIA PERRY:

Homunculus. New York: CF. (CFI, Composers, Recordings, Inc. , S-252)

Short Piece for Orchestra. (CRI 1451)

Stabat Mater. (CRI 133)

Pittman, Evelyn La Rue. Rich Heritage: Songs, Stories, Pictures, Vol. 1. New White Plains, N. Y. : Rich Heritage Co. , 1968.

_____. "Rock-a-My Soul." New York: Carl Fischer, 1952. (for baritone and five-part chorus)

Price, Florence B. "Adoration." Dayton, Ohio: Lorenz. (for organ)

_____. "Anticipation (La anticipacion)." One of five easy compositions for piano by Florence B. Price. Chicago: McKinley Music Co. , 1928. (Publ. pl. no. 2241)

_____. "An April Day." Words by Joseph F. Colte. New York: Handy Bros. , 1949.

_____. "Bright Eyes." Bryn Mawr, Pa. : Theodore Presser, 1937.

_____. "The Butterfly." From Pieces We Like to Play, ed. by Gail Martin Haake, Charles J. Haake, and

Osborne McConathy.   New York: Carl Fischer, 1936.

_____.   "Cabin Song."   Bryn Mawr, Pa. :   Theodore Pres-
ser, 1937.

_____.   "Concert Overture No. 1."   Based on Negro
spirituals.   10 min.

_____.   "Concert Overture No. 2."   Based on three Negro
spirituals.   12 min.

_____.   Concerto for Piano and Orchestra.   One move-
ment.   16 min.

_____.   Concerto in D Major.   16 min.   (for violin and
orchestra)

_____.   "Criss Cross ... Rock-a-Bye."   Chicago: Mc-
Kinley Publishers, Inc.

_____.   Dances in the Canebrakes.   Based on authentic
Negro rhythms.   Los Angeles: Affiliated Musicians,
Inc.   (for piano)

_____.   Dances in the Canebrakes.   Suite.   New York:
Mills.

_____.   "Doll Waltz (Vals de la musica)."   One of five
easy compositions for piano by Florence B. Price.
Chicago: McKinley Music Co. , 1928.   (Publ. pl. no.
2242)

_____.   "The Engine (La maquine de vapor)."   One of five
easy compositions for piano.   Chicago: McKinley Music
Co. , 1928.   (Publ. pl. no. 2243)   Grade 2.

_____.   "The Goblin and the Mosquito."   Chicago: SUM.
(for piano)

_____.   "The Gnat and the Bee."   From Pieces We Like
to Play.   New York: Carl Fischer.

_____.   "Heav'n Bound Soldier."   New York: Handy Bros.,
1949.   Arr. by Florence B. Price.   (Negro spiritual for
women's voices)

_____.   "Here and There."   Chicago: McKinley.   (piano
solo)

_____. "Hoe Cake." From Three Little Negro Dances. Bryn Mawr, Pa. : Theodore Presser. (two scores for two pianos)

_____. "I Am Bound for the Kingdom." In Two Traditional Negro Spirituals. New York: Handy Bros.

_____. "I'm Workin' on My Building." In Two Traditional Negro Spirituals. New York: Handy Bros.

_____. "In Quiet Mood." Chicago: Summy; New York: Galaxy. (for organ)

_____. "Little Negro Dances." Bryn Mawr, Pa. : Theodore Presser, 1939. (Arr. for band)

_____. "March of the Beetles ... Clover Blossom." Chicago: McKinley, 1947. (for piano)

_____. "Mississippi River." 10 min.

_____. "The Moon Bridge." Words by Mary Rolofson Gamble. Chicago: Gamble, Hinged Music Co. , 1930.

_____. "Morning Sunbeam." Bryn Mawr, Pa. : Theodore Presser, 1937.

_____. "Nature's Magic." Secular choral music. Words by Mary Rolofson Gamble. Chicago: Summy. (for treble voices)

_____. "The Oak." Tone poem.

_____. "The Old Boatman." Chicago: Summy. (a piano solo)

_____. "Rabbit Foot." From Three Little Negro Dances. Bryn Mawr, Pa. : Theodore Presser. (two scores for two pianos)

_____. "The Rose." New York: Carl Fischer, 1936. (piano solo, grade 3)

_____. "A Sachem's Pipe." New York: Carl Fischer, 1935. (Grade 3)

_____. "The Sea Swallow." Chicago: Summy. (piano solo)

_____. "Sonata in E Minor." 1959. (piano)

_____. "Songs to a Dark Virgin." Lyrics by Langston Hughes. New York: G. Schirmer.

_____. Suite No. 1. 1959. (for organ)

_____. Symphony in C Minor. Four movements. 22 min.

_____. Symphony in D Minor. Four movements. 20 min.

_____. Symphony in E Minor. Four movements. 20 min.

_____. Symphony in G Minor. 25 min.

_____. "Tecumseh." New York: Carl Fischer, 1935. (Grade 3)

_____. "Ticklin' Toes." From Three Little Negro Dances. Bryn Mawr, Pa.: Theodore Presser. (two scores for two pianos)

_____. Two Traditional Spirituals. New York: Handy Bros., 1948.

_____. "The Waltzing Fairy (El duende valsante)." One of five easy compositions for piano. Chicago: McKinley Music Co., 1928. (Publ. pl. no. 2244)

_____. "The Waterfall (La cascada)." One of five easy compositions for piano. Chicago: McKinley Music Co., 1928. (for piano, grade 2)

_____. "Witch of the Meadow." Words by Mary R. Gamble. Chicago: Gamble, Hinged Music Co. (SSA)

_____. "The Zephry (El Cafiro)." Mexican folk song. Transcribed for piano. Chicago: McKinley Co., 1938. (Grade 3. Publ. pl. no. 2279)

RECORDING OF FLORENCE B. PRICE:

"My Soul's Been Anchored in de Lord." London: LPS-182 (Ellabelle Davis, soprano), Victor, 1799.

Rainey, Gertrude ("Ma"). "Boweavil Blues." Northern Music Corp., 1924.

_____. "Broken Hearted Blues." Northern Music Corp.,
1929.

_____. "Counting the Blues." Northern Music Corp.,
1929.

_____. "Deep Moaning Blues." Northern Music Corp.,
1928.

_____. "Hear Me Talkin' to You." Northern Music Corp.,
1928.

_____. "See See Rider." New York: Leeds Music Corp.,
1934, 1944.

RECORDINGS OF GERTRUDE RAINEY:

"Blame It on the Blues." Milestone, 2008.

"Blues the World Forgot." Biograph, 12001.

"Bo Weavil Blues." Riverside, RL 8007.

"Cellbound Blues." Milestone, MLP 2001.

"Counting the Blues." Riverside, RPP 12-101, microgroove.

"Immortal Ma Rainey." Milestone, 2001.

"Ma and Pa's Poorhouse Blues." Audubon AAM.

"On My Babe Blues." Biograph, 12011.

"Queen of the Blues." Biograph, 12032.

"See See Rider." Riverside, RLP 1001.

Rainey, Gertrude ("Ma") and J. Mayo Williams. "Titanic
Man Blues." Northern Music Corp., 1926.

Reagon, Bernice. "Matriarch Blues." In The Sound of Thunder. Atlanta, Georgia: Kin Tell Corporation, 1200
Spring Street, N.W. 30309.

Schuyler, Philippa Duke. African Rhapsody. 1965.

_____. Around the World Suite. 1960.

_____. Chisamharu the Nogomo (Mozambique). Premiered
at the New York Town Hall, Sunday, Sept. 13, 1964.

_____. "Country Boy." Arr. by Juan Hines. 1957.

_____. "Cynthia." With Juan Hines. 1957.

_____. The Legend of Mahdi. 1965.

_____. Manhattan Nocturne. Scored for 100-piece sym-
phony, 1943. Premiered by the New York Philharmonic
Orchestra, Carnegie Hall. First-prize composition in
Grinnell Foundation Contest, Detroit, Michigan. Also
performed by the Chicago and San Francisco Symphonies.

_____. "New Moon." Arr. by Philippa Schuyler and John
Kelly, 1950.

_____. The Nile Fantasy: 1. "Inshallah, or Fate ...
Contemplation and Submission"; 2. "Violence and Ter-
ror"; 3. "The Long Road to Peace." (for piano and
orchestra) Premiered in Cairo, Egypt by the Cairo
Symphony Orchestra with Miss Schuyler as soloist, December 10, 1965. Premiered in America at a memorial recital for Miss Schuyler, September 24, 1967,
Leonard De Paur, conductor. Margaret Bonds, arranger.

_____. The Rhapsody of Youth. Premiered in Port au
Prince, Haiti, 1948. Miss Schuyler received the Medal
of Merit and Honor from President Paul E. Magliore
for this composition.

_____. Rumpelstiltsken. Scherzo from her Fairytale
Symphony. Composed and orchestrated by Philippa
Duke Schuyler. Premiered by the New York Philhar-
monic Orchestra, 1944. Also played by the Boston
Pops and Cincinnati Symphony.

_____. Rumpelstiltsken. Para piano, musica and ar-
rangement de Philippa Duke Schuyler. Buenos Aires:
Ricordi Americana. (12pp.)

_____. Sleepy Hollow Sketches. 1946. The piano trans-
scription premiered at United Nations celebration,

Tarrytown on the Hudson, birthplace of Washington Irving. Later, played by the New York Junior Symphony
Orchestra and at the Fisk Musical Festival. Also an
award-winning composition.

_____. Three Little Pieces. Nov. 10, 1938.

_____. The White Nile Suite. 1954. Musical saga de-
picting Arab history in Egypt and the Sudan. (for piano
solo)

RECORDING OF PHILIPPA DUKE SCHUYLER:

International Favorites: Philippa Schuyler, pianist.
Mono Vol. I. Middle Tone Records, Emanuel A. Mid-
dleton Music Publishers, 1576 Broadway, New York
10036.

Simone, Nina. "Compensation." Words by Paul L. Dunbar.
New York: Rolls Royce Music.

_____. "Nobody." New York: Sam Fox, 1964.

_____. "Real-Real." New York: Rolls Royce Co.

_____. "Revolution." With Weldon Irvine, Jr. Mt. Ver-
non, N. Y. : Ninandy Music Co.

_____. "To Be Young, Gifted and Black." Arr. H. Smith.
Mt. Vernon, N. Y. : Ninandy Music Co. (mixed SATB
voices)

Simpson, Valerie and Nickolas Ashford. Tear It on Down.
Erva Music Publishing Co. , Inc.

Smith, Bessie. "Baby Doll." Gus Kahn Music Co. , 1927.

_____. "Dixie Flyer Blues." Empress Music Inc. , 1925.

_____. "Don't Fish in My Sea." Northern Music Corp. ,
1928.

_____. "Reckless Blues." C. R. Publishing Co. , 1925.

RECORDINGS OF BESSIE SMITH:

"Any Woman's Blues." Columbia, G30126.

"The Bessie Smith Story." Columbia, CL 88578.

"Empress." Columbia, G30818.

"Empty Bed Blues." Columbia, G30450.

"World's Greatest Blues Singer." Columbia, GP 33.

Smith, Bessie and Gertrude "Ma" Rainey. "Weeping Woman Blues." Northern Music Corp.

Smith, Bessie and Clarence Williams. "Jail House Blues." MCA, Inc. and Empress Music Inc., 1924.

Smith, Clara. "Black Woman's Blues." Mayfair Music Corp., 1927.

_____, and Stanley S. Miller. "Every Woman's Blues." Mills.

Smith, Mamie and Porter Grainger. "Plain Old Blues." Mills, 1923.

Spivey, Victoria. "T. B. Blues." Mayfair Music Corp., 1927.

Stallworth, Dottie C. "All People Can Live Together." Composer.

_____. "Christmas Time Bossonova." Composer.

_____. "Creativity Children." Composer.

_____. "Get It Together." Composer.

_____. "Guide Me, Jesus." In Religious Education Series. Morristown, N. J.: Silver-Burdett, 1976.

_____. "His Spirit of Love." In Religious Education Series. Silver-Burdett, 1976.

_____. "I Hear Sounds." Silver-Burdett, 1977.

_____. "Let's Keep What We Have for Tomorrow." Composer.

_____. "Love Everybody Wherever You Go." Composer.

Dottie C. Stallworth

_____. "Make the World a Better Place." Silver-Burdett,
1976.

_____. "Spread It All Around." Composer.

_____. "'Tis Spring." Composer.

_____. "Trust in God." Silver-Burdett, 1977.

_____. "Turn Back Your Thermostat." Commercial re-
cording. Public Services: Electric and Gas, New Jersey, New York, Philadelphia.

_____. "'Twill Be a Rocking Christmas." Composer.

_____. "We Ought to Live Like Grandma Lived: She
Didn't Have Pollution." Composer.

_____. "What's Keeping Us from Being Me and You?"
Composer.

RECORDING OF DOTTIE C. STALLWORTH AND TRIO:

"I Wish I Knew How it Feels to Be Free," and "Wave."
Art Records, 685 15th Ave., Irvington, N.J.

Taylor, Maude Cummings. "The Day Is Nearly Done."
Spiritual. New York: Handy Bros. (for voice and
piano)

Thomas, Carla. "Gee Whiz!" East Publications, 1960.
Atlantic Records.

Thorpe, Sister Rosetta (also: Tharpe). "Strange Things Are
Happening Every Day." Decca, 1958.

_____. "Up Above My Head, I Hear Music in the Air."
New York: Montauk Music Inc.

Waters, Ethel, Fletcher Henderson and Lewis Mitchell. "Kind
Lovin' Blues." Mills.

_____, and Sidney Easton. "Maybe Not at All." C. R.
Publishing Co., 1925.

Wilburn, LaVilla Tullos. "Dear Miss Minnie," and "Green,
Green, Rocky Road." In Afro-America Sings, ed. by

Ollie McFarland and others. Detroit: Borad of Education, 1971.

_____. "Goodnight, Donna Jean, Goodnight." In Afro-America Sings.

_____. "There Was a Babe." In Afro-America Sings.

_____. "There You Are." In Afro-America Sings.

_____. "This Is My Land." Words, Langston Hughes. In Afro-America Sings.

_____. "This Is the Christmas Time." In Afro-America Sings.

_____. "Who Has Seen America?" Words by Ollie McFarland. In Afro-America Sings.

Williams, Mary Lou. "Camel Hop." New York: Robbins Music Co.

_____. "Glory to God."

_____. "In the Land of OO-bla-dee." New York: Capital Songs. Copyright Criterion Music Corp.

_____. "Just an Idea." Jewell Music Publ. Co., Inc.

_____. "Lonely Moments." New York: Harman Music Co., Inc. Arr. Mary Lou Williams and Milton Orent. Piano conductor score (orchestra and parts).

_____. Mass.

_____. Mass of the Lenten Season.

_____. Mary Lou's Mass. Performed at City Center Theater, New York, March 1972. Performed by Alvin Ailey American Dance Theater. Mary Lou Williams, conductor.

_____. New American Music. New York Section Composers of the 1970s. Volumes 1-3. Folkways, FTS 33901-3.

_____. "Nursery Rhymes No. 2."

_____. "Roll 'Em." New York: Robbins Music Co.

RECORDINGS OF MARY LOU WILLIAMS:

Kansas City Jazz. Decca (A)DL 8044.

A Keyboard History. Jazztone 1206.

Storyville 906 ("Messin' 'Round in Montmartre").

Williams, Mary Lou, William Johnston, and Leo Mosley.
"Pretty-Eyed Baby." Pickwick Music Corp., 1951.

_____, Jack Lawrence, and Paul Webster. "What's
Your Story, Morning Glory." Advanced Music Corp.

_____, and others. An Evening with Scott Joplin. New
York Public Library, 1972 (a gift of Nonesuch Records).
Soloist and chorus, with piano accompaniment. John
Motley, Director.

Williams, Thelma O. (Iola Bolles). "The Alphabet," "Columbus," "Let's Build a Tower," "The Little Fish,"
"Move Like This," and "The Old Man." In The Grow-
ing with Music Series, K-6. Englewood Cliffs, N.J.:
Prentice Hall, 1972.

c) Other Musical Recordings

Addison, Adele. Twelve Poems of Emily Dickinson, Aaron
Copeland. (Three choruses.) CBS Masterworks. 32
110017, 1967. 2 s, 12 in., 33-1/3.

Arroyo, Martina. Andromache's Farewell by Samuel
Barber. Columbia ML 5912. 1963. New York
Philharmonic.
_____. Judas Maccabaeus, Georg Friedrich Handel.
Westminster XWL 3310. 1959. Also with Grace Bum-
bry.

_____. Momente, Karlheing Stockhousen. Nonesuch Re-
cords, H 71157. 1967.

_____. Requiem, Op. 48, Gabriel Urban Faure. Decca
DL 710169. 1970.

_____. Stabat Mater, Gioacchino Antonis Rosina. Colum-
bia ML 6142. 1965.

_____. Symphony No. 9, Op. 125, D Minor, Ludvig Van
Beethoven. Columbia, M2S 794(MS7211-7212) 1969.

_____, and others. La Juive, Halevy. New Philharmonia
Orchestra, Antonion de Almeida, conductor. Ambrosian
Opera Chorus, John McCarthy, Director. RCA, ARL-
1-0447 Stereo, Red Seal.

Bumbry, Grace. Don Carlo, Giuseppe Verdi. Libretti by
Mey and DuLocles. Seraphim IC 6004. 1964. 6S, 12
in. 33-1/3 rpm, microgroove.

_____. Judas Maccabaeus, Georg Friedrich Handel. (Eng-
lish Phonodisc.) Westminster WXL3310. 1950. 6S,
12 in. 33-1/3 rpm, microgroove. Also, Martina Arroyo.

_____. Messiah, Georg Friedrich Handel. (Complete
version, original instrumentation.) Ed. Herbage. London, A 4357(X. 5665-5667.) 1966. Also, Joan Suther-
land.

Elam, Dorothy Conley and Lavinia A. Franklin. Historical
Interpretation of Negro Spirituals and Lift Every Voice
and Sing. Camden, N.J.: Recorded Publications, n.d.

Fitzgerald, Ella. Ella Fitzgerald Sings the Duke Ellington
Song Book. HMV CLP 1213-14.

Franklin, Aretha. Aretha Now. Atlantic Stereo, SD 8788.

Handy, D. Antoinette. Contemporary Black Images in Music for Flute. The Trio Pro Viva and Gladys P. Norris, piano; Ronald Lipscomb, cello. Music of ten contemporary Black composers represented through eleven
different compositions for solo flute; solo alto flute;
flute, cello, and piano; flute and cello; and flute, violin
and piano.

_____, Trio Pro Viva. Contemporary Black Images in
Music for the Flute. Joseph Kennedy, violin; Ronald

Lipscomb, cello; Gladys Norris, piano; William Terry, piano. Eastern ERS-513.

Hinderas, Natalie. Natalie Hinderas Plays Music by Black Composers. Desto Records, Lake Record Sales Corp., Franklin Lakes, N.J. 12-inch LP.

Perry, Julia. Homunculus. Composers Recordings CRI SD 252. 1970. Microgroove, stereophonic.

_____. A Short Piece. For orchestra. Composers Recordings CRI 145. 1961. 12 min. microgroove. Imperial Philharmonic of Tokyo, William Strickland, conductor. Duration 7 min., 10 sec.

_____. Stabat Mater. Composers Recordings CRI 133. 1960. 12 in. 33-1/3 rpm., microgroove. For contralto and string orchestra. Makiko Asakuro, mezzo-soprano, William Strickland, conductor.

Price, Leontyne. Aida, Giuseppi Verdi. Libretto, Antonia Chislonzoni. RCA Victor, LM 6158. 1962. 6 s, 12-1/2, 33-1/3 rpm, microgroove. Also Rita Gorr, Dan Vickers, Robert Merrill, Giorgio Tizz. Rome Opera House and Chorus. George Solti, conductor.

_____. Hermit Songs, Samuel Barber. Columbia ML 4988. 1955. 1 s, 12 in., 33-1/3 rpm., microgroove. American Music Series.

_____. Prima Donna, Volume 3. Great Soprano Arias from Gluck to Poulenc. London Symphony Orchestra, Edward Downes, conductor. RCA, LBC-3163, Stereo.

Schuyler, Philippa. International Favorites. Vol. I, Mono, LP. Middle-Tone Records, 1576 Broadway, N.Y. 10036.

Smith, Undine (Moore). Undine Smith Moore Song Book. Virginia State College Concert Choir, Dr. Carl Harris, Jr., conductor. Rich-sound Records, 4112N10 (Afro-American Heritage Series, vol. 3). Available through Virginia State College, Box 352, Petersburg, Va.

Verrett-Carter, Shirley. Lucrezia Borgia, Gaetano Donizetti. Libretto, Felici Romani, based on Victor Hugo's play Lucrezia Borgia. RCA Victor, LSC 6176. 1967. 6 s,

12 in. , 33-1/3 rpm microgroove. Stereophonic. Also
Montserrat Caballi, Alfredo Kraus, and Ezio Flagillo.
RCA. Italian Opera Orchestra and Chorus, Jonel Per-
lea, conductor.

_____. Shirley Verrett Carnegie Hall Recital. RCA Vic-
tor LM 2835. 1965. 2 x, 12 in. 33-1/3 rpm, microgroove.

17. AUDIO-VISUAL MATERIALS

a) Films By or Based on Black Women's Works

Anderson, Marian. Marian Anderson. Concerts in Film
Series (WAI). 27 min. RS-363.

Angelou, Maya. Georgia, Georgia. Cinema Releasing. St.
Louis, Mo.

Black on Black. Individual films on Shirley Chisholm and
Coretta King and others. Produced and distributed by
Timelli, 1971. 60 min. Rental $7.50. Purchase $50.

Blue, Carroll Parrott. Two Women. 10 min. Shown at
Filmex Film Festival, 1977. (Monologue during which
and old Black woman and a young Black woman share
traumatic experiences that help to influence the direction
of their lives.)

Delta Sigma Theta Sorority. Count Down at Kusini. Distributed by Columbia Pictures, 1976.

Franklin, Aretha. Aretha Franklin, Soul Singer. McGraw-
Hill Films, 330 W. 42nd St., N.Y. 10036. 25 min.
Rental $25.00. Purchase $325. In color.

Hansberry, Lorraine. A Raisin in the Sun. Audio-Film
Center, 2138 E. 75th St., Mt. Vernon, N.Y. 10550.
127 min. Rental $25.00.

Hunter, Kristin. The Landlord. United Artists, N.Y.

Mantell, Harold. Lorraine Hansberry: The Black Experience
in the Creation of Drama. 35 min., color, 1975. Dis-
tributior: Films for the Humanities, P.O. Box 2053,
Princeton, N.J.

Tubman, Harriet. Harriet Tubman. Society for Visual Education, Inc. , 1345 Diversey Parkway, Chicago, 60614.

Vroman, Mary Elizabeth. A Bright Road. M-G-M.

b) Cassette Tapes

Arnez, Nancy and Beatrice Murphy. The Rocks Cry Out.
Detroit: Broadside. $5. 00.

Brooks, Gwendolyn. Gwendolyn Brooks Reading Her Poems
with Comment. January 19, 1961. Library of Congress
109 LW 3237.

_____, and Peter Viereck. A joint reading by the two
poets at the YMHA Poetry Center, New York. Library
of Congress 110 LWO 2863. Reel 2.

Burrows, Vinnie. Vinnie Burrows. Production Listening Library, Inc. , 1 Park Ave. , Greenwich, Conn. 06870.

Danner, Margaret and Dudley Randall. Poem Counterpoem.
Detroit: Broadside. $5. 00.

Giovanni, Nikki. Nikki Giovanni Reads Re: Creation. Detroit: Broadside. $5. 00.

Sanchez, Sonia. Sonia Sanchez Reads "Homecoming. " Detroit: Broadside. $5. 00.

Stephany. Stephany Reads "Moving Deep. " Detroit: Broadside. $5. 00.

Walker, Margaret. Prophets for a New Day. Detroit:
Broadside. $5. 00.

c) Records

Angelou, Maya. The Poetry of Maya Angelou. GWP Records
ST 20001.

Brooks, Gwendolyn. "Kitchenette," "Song of the Yard," "The
    Preacher Ruminates," "The Children of the Poor,"
    "Old Laughter," and "Beverly Hills, Chicago." Antho-
    logy of Negro Poets, Folkway Records, FL 9791.

Burroughs, Margaret G.   What Shall I Tell My Children Who
    Are Black?   Sound-A-Rama SOR 101 2S 12.

Davis, Angela.   Soul and Soledad.   Flying Dutchman Produc-
    tions. ATCO Records, 1841 Broadway, New York 10023.
    Stereo FD 10141.

Giovanni, Nikki.   Truth Is on Its Way.   Right-on Records
    15001.

Hansberry, Lorraine.   Lorraine Hansberry on Her Art and
    the Black Experience (discussing her work and philoso-
    phy, the theater, the Black experience, and the chal-
    lenge of the artist in mid-century America). New York:
    Caedmon Records, TC 1352, 12 in. LP, $6.50; CDL
    51352 cassette, $7.95.

_____. Lorraine Hansberry Speaks Out: Art and the Black
    Revolution. Sel. and ed. by Robert Nemiroff. New
    York: Caedmon Records, 1971.

_____. A Raisin in the Sun.   (The complete play, 3 re-
    cords with Ossie Davis, Ruby Dee, Claudia McNeil,
    Diana Sands, Leonard Jackson, Zakes Mokae, Sam
    Schacht, Harold Scott. Directed by Lloyd Richards.)
    New York: Caedmon Records, 1972.

_____. To Be Young, Gifted and Black.   (The complete
    play, 3 records with James Earl Jones, Barbara Bax-
    ley, Claudia McNeil, Tina Sattin, Camille Yarbrough,
    Garn Stevens, John Towey.) New York: Caedmon Re-
    cords, 1971.

Historical Interpretation of Negro Spirituals and "Lift Every
    Voice and Sing." Dorothy Conley Elam, researcher and
    narrator. Lavinia A. Franklin, organist. Camden,
    N.J.: Recorded Publications Co.; write Mrs. Dorothy
    Elam, Rt. 2, Box 371 C, Berlin, N.J. 08009.

Hughes, Langston and Margaret Danner. "Writers of the
    Revolution." Black Forum, H-1725, Motown Record
    Corp.

Jenkins, Ella. "And One and Two, " and Other Songs. Folk-
    way Records, FC 7544, 701 Seventh Ave., New York.

_____. Early Early Childhood Songs. Scholastic Records,
    FC 7630.

_____. "My Street Begins at My House," and Other Songs
    and Rhythms from the "Me Too Show." Folkways Re-
    cords, FC 7543.

King, Coretta Scott. Coretta Scott King Reads from "My Life
    with Martin Luther King." New York: Caedmon Re-
    cords TC 2060 2-12 in. LPs, $13.00.

_____. Free at Last! Free at Last! New York: Caed-
    mon, TC 1407.

_____. The Freedom Movement. New York: Caedmon,
    TC 1406.

_____. My Life with Martin Luther King, Jr. New York:
    Caedmon, TC 9300.

Kitt, Eartha and Moses Gunn. Black Pioneers in American
    History (19th century), Vol. 1.   (Reading the autobio-
    graphies of Charlotte Forten, Frederick Douglass, Susie
    King Taylor, and Nat Love.) New York: Caedmon Re-
    cords, Inc. , TC 1252 1 12 in. LP, $6.50; CDL 51252
    cassette, $7.25.

The Negro Woman. Produced by Listening Library, Inc. , 1
    Park Ave. , New York 10036. Purchase Price $5.79.

Reagon, Bernice. The Sound of Thunder. Atlanta: Kin-Tel
    Recording Studios.

Sands, Diana and Moses Gunn. Black Pioneers in American
    History (19th-20th century), Vol. 2. (Reading the auto-
    biographies of Mary Church Terrell, W. E. B. DuBois,
    Josiah Henson, and William Parker.) New York: Caed-
    mon Records, TC 1299 1 12 in. LP, $6.50; CDL 51244
    cassette, $7.95.

Shange, Ntozoke. For Colored Girls Who Have Considered
    Suicide /When the Rainbow Is Enuf! Original Cast Re-
    cordings, Shakespeare Festival Productions. Produced
    by Oz Scott, Herbert Harris, Frank Kulaga. Buddah
    Records, 1969.

Walker, Margaret. "For My People," "Old Molly Means,"
"Kissie Lee," "Stackalee," "John Henry." Anthology
of Negro Poets, Folkways Records, FL 9791.

d) Video Tapes

Madgett, Naomi. Naomi Madgett, Donald Hall, and Dan Ger-
ber Reading Their Poems and Talking to Students.
Michigan Council for the Arts, 10215 E. Jefferson Ave.,
Detroit 48214.

Robert Hayden, Naomi Madgett, and Dudley Randall Read the
Six Poems They Want to Be Remembered by.   8mm
Black and White. 50 min. Rental. Oakland Community
College, Orchard Lake, Mich. 48030.

The Role of the Black Woman in America. Discussion by
four Black women: Peachie Brooks, Verta S. Grosvenor,
Flo Kennedy, Elinor Norton. Pacifica Tape Library,
2217 Shattuck St., Berkeley, Calif. 94704. 50 min.
Purchase price $10.50.

PART II

SELECTED INDIVIDUAL BIBLIOGRAPHIES

Maya Angelou

SELECTED INDIVIDUAL BIBLIOGRAPHY

MAYA ANGELOU

BOOKS

Gather Together in My Name. New York: Random House, 1974.

I Know Why the Caged Bird Sings. New York: Random House, 1969.

Just Give Me a Cool Drink of Water 'fore I Die. New York: Random House, 1971.

O Pray My Wings Are Gonna Fit Me Well. New York: Random House, 1975.

Singin' and Swingin' and Gettin' Merry Like Christmas. New York: Random House, 1976.

PLAYS

Adjoa A Missah, 1967.

And Still I Rise, to open in New York in Spring, 1977.

The Best of These, 1966.

The Clawing Within, 1966-67.

AUDIO-VISUALS

Georgia, Georgia. Cinema Releasing, St. Louis, Mo. (The first movie screenplay by a Black woman.)

The Poetry of Maya Angelou. GWP Records. ST 20001.

143

BIOGRAPHY AND CRITICISM

Bogle, Donald. Toms, Coons, Mulattos, Mammie, and Bucks. New York: Viking Press, 1973.

Butterfield, Stephen. Black Autobiography in America. New York: University of Massachusetts Press, 1974.

"I Know Why the Caged Bird Sings," Ebony 25:4 (April, 1970), 62-64.

Julianelli, J. "Angelou: Interview," Harper's Bazaar, November, 1972, p. 124.

Krier, Beth Ann. "Maya Angelou: No Longer a 'Caged Bird,'" View Section, Los Angeles Times, Friday, September 24, 1976, pp. 1, 8, 9.

Patterson, Lindsay. Black Films and Film Makers. New York: Dodd, Mead and Company, 1975.

Shockley, Ann and Sue Chandler. Living Black American Authors: A Biographical Directory. Foreword by Jessie Carney Smith. R. R. Bowker Co., 1973.

Smith, Sidonie Ann. "The Song of a Caged Bird: Maya Angelou's Quest for Self-Acceptance," Southern Humanities Review 7 (Fall, 1973), 365-374.

"Viva Interview: Maya Angelou: Author, Civil Rights Leader, Film Director," Viva 1:6 (March, 1974), 62-63, 96, 99, 102.

Weller, Sheila. "Work in Progress: Maya Angelou," Intellectual Digest 3 (June, 1973), 1.

GWENDOLYN BROOKS

BOOKS

Annie Allen. New York: Harper, 1949.

The Bean Eaters. New York: Harper, 1960.

Bronzeville Boys and Girls. New York: Harper, 1966.

A Capsule Course in Black Poetry Writing. Detroit: Broad-
    side, 1975.

Family Pictures. Detroit: Broadside, 1970.

In the Mecca. New York: Harper and Row, 1968.

Jump Bad. Presented by Gwendolyn Brooks. Detroit:
    Broadside, 1971.

Maude Martha. New York: Harper, 1953.

Riot. Detroit: Broadside, 1969.

Selected Poems. New York: Harper and Row, 1963.

A Street in Bronzeville. New York: Harper, 1945.

The Tiger Who Wore Gloves. Chicago: Third World, 1974.

We Asked Gwendolyn Brooks. Interview by Paul Angle.
    Chicago: Illinois Bell Telephone Co. , 1967.

The World of Gwendolyn Brooks. New York: Harper and
    Row, 1971. (Poems and novel)

ARTICLES

Introduction. Don't Scream, by Don L. Lee. Detroit:
    Broadside, 1969.

"Langston Hughes. " (Editorial.) Nation 205 (July 3, 1967), 7.

AUDIO-VISUALS

Brooks, Gwendolyn and Peter Viereck. A Joint Reading by
    the Two Poets at the YMHA Poetry Center, New York
    City. Library of Congress 110 LWO 2863, Reel 2.

Family Pictures. Detroit: Broadside, $5. 00 (tape).

Gwendolyn Brooks Reading Her Poems with Comment. Janu-
    ary 19, 1961. Library of Congress 109 LWO 3237 (tape).

Gwendolyn Brooks Reading Her Poetry.   Introductory Poem
by Don L. Lee.   Caedmon TC 1244.

"Kitchenette" and other poems.   Anthology of Negro Poets.
Folkway Records FL 9791.

BIOGRAPHY AND CRITICISM

Adams, Russell.   Great Negroes Past and Present.   Illus.
by Eugene Einslow.   Chicago: Afro-Am Pub. Co. , 1964.

Brown, Frank London.   "Chicago's Great Lady of Poetry,"
Negro Digest 11 (December 1961), 53-57.

Contemporary Authors.   Vol. I (1962).

Crockett, J.   "An Essay on Gwendolyn Brooks," Negro History Bulletin 19 (1955), 37-39.

Current Biography (1950).

Cutler, B.   "Long Reach, Strong Speech," Poetry 103 (1954),
388-389.

Davis, Arthur P.   "The Black-and-Tan Motif in the Poetry of
Gwendolyn Brooks," CLA Journal 6 (1962), 90-97.

_____.   "Gwendolyn Brooks: A Poet of the Unheroic,"
CLA Journal 7 (December 1963), 114-125.

Emanuel, James A.   "A Note on the Future of Negro Poetry,"
Negro American Literature Forum 1 (Fall 1967), 2-3.

Jaffee, Dan.   "Gwendolyn Brooks: An Appreciation from the
White Suburbs. "   In The Black American Writer, II:
Poetry and Drama, ed. by C. W. E. Bigsby.   Balti-
more: Penguin Books, 1969.

Kent, George.   "The Poetry of Gwendolyn Brooks, " Parts 1
and 2, Black World 20:11 (September 1971), 36-48;
20:12 (October 1971), 30-42.

Kunitz, Stanley.   "Bronze by Gold," Poetry 76 (1950), 52-56.

Rollins, Charlemae.   Famous American Negro Poets.   New
York: Dodd, Mead, 1965.

Twentieth Century Authors. 1st suppl. (1955).

ELIZABETH CATLETT (PAINTER AND SCULPTOR)

PRINTS

(Prints listed here, in chronological order, came from the
   Elizabeth Catlett catalogue, Studio Museum, Harlem)

"Black Is Beautiful III," 1957. Lithograph. 13 x 13-1/2.

"Pan [Bread]." Linocut. 17-1/2 x 23 in.

"Indian Woman." 1958. Lithograph. 13-1/2 x 16-1/4 in.

"Newsboy." 1958. Lithograph. 10 x 12-5/8 in.

"Vendedora de Periodicus [Newspaper seller]," 1958. Lithograph. 17-3/4 x 23 in.

"Shoeshine Boy," 1958. Lithograph. 23 x 17-3/4 in.

"Skipping Boy," 1958. Lithograph. 17-5/8 x 23 in.

"Black Maternity," 1959. Lithography. 16 x 21-1/2 in.

"Rafaela," 1959. Seriograph. 9-1/4 x 13-3/4 in.

"Habla la Mujer Negro [The Black Woman Speaks]," 1960.
   Lithograph. 27-1/2 x 18-3/4 in.

Sirvienta [Servant]," 1962. Linocut. 13 x 10 in.

"Mujeres de America [Women of America]," 1963. Woodcut.
   13-3/4 x 18-3/4 in.

"Latin America Dice 'No'!" 1968. Linocut. 22 x 23-1/2 in.

"Negro es Bello I [Black Is Beautiful]," 1968. Lithograph.
   13 x 20 in.

"Rebozos," 1968. Lithograph. 20 x 13 in.

"Malcolm X Speaks for Us," 1969. Linocut. 37-1/2 x
   27-3/4 in.

"The Torture of Mothers," 1970.   Lithograph.   13 x 20 in.

"Watts/Detroit/Washington/Harlem/Newark," 1970.   Linocut.
27-3/4 x 37-1/2 in.

SCULPTURE

Rebozo IV, 1965.   Bronze.   11 in.   Dr. and Mrs. J. P.
Jones, New York City.

Olmec Bather, 1967.   Bronze.   22 in.   The Artist.

Pensive Figure, 1967.   Bronze.   22 in.   Mr. and Mrs. Har-
vey Rambach, New York City.

Rebozo II, 1967.   Cast Stone.   13-3/16 in.   The Artist.

Black Unity, 1968.   Cedar.   20-1/2 x 24 in.   The Brockman
Gallery, Los Angeles.

Homage to My Young Black Sisters, 1969.   Cedar.   7-1/2 in.
The Artist.

Nude Torso, 1969.   Bronze.   13-3/4 in.   The Artist.

The Black Woman Speaks.   1970.   Tropical Wood.   16-1/8
in.   Brockman Gallery, Los Angeles.

Recognition, 1970.   Black onyx.   16-1/2 in.   The Artist.

Pregnancy, 1970.   Walnut.   33 in.   Brockman Gallery, Los
Angeles.

Target Practice, 1970.   Bronze.   13-1/2 in.   The Artist.

Magic Mask, 1971.   Mahogany.   10-5/8 in.   The Artist.

Mother and Child, 1971.   Cedar.   26 in.   Brockman Gallery.

Political Prisoner, 1971.   Cedar.   71-1/4 in.   The Artist.

Sister, 1971.   Green Marble.   13 in.   The Artist.

ALICE CHILDRESS

BOOKS

Black Scenes, editor. New York: Doubleday, 1971.

Gold Through the Trees. 1952 (unpublished).

Like One of the Family. Brooklyn: Independence Publishers,
     1956.

Martin Luther King at Montgomery, Alabama. 1969 (unpub-
     lished).

Trouble in Mind. 1955 (mimeo copy in possession of author).

Wine in the Wilderness. (Dramatist Play Service).

OTHER PLAYS

"Florence: A One Act Drama," Masses and Mainstream 3
     (October 1950), 34-47.

"Mojo: A Black Love Story," Black World 20:6 (April 1971),
     54-82.

SHORT STORIES

"The Health Card." Harlem, U.S.A., ed. and intro., by John
     Henrik Clarke. Berlin: Seven Seas Publishers, 1964.

"I Go to a Funeral." Harlem, U.S.A.

ARTICLES

"A Woman Playwright Speaks Her Mind." Freedomways 6
     (1966), 75-80.

BIOGRAPHY AND CRITICISM

Evans, Donald. "Bring It All Back Home," Black World 20:4
     (February 1971), 41-45.

EUGENIA COLLIER

BOOKS

Collier, Eugenia, Joel Glasser, Edward Meyers, George
Steele, and Thomas L. Wolf. A Bridge to Saying It
Well. Springfield, Va.: Norvec Publishing Co., 1970.
(Freshman textbook)

_____, and Richard Long. Afro-American Writing: Prose
and Poetry. New York: New York University Press,
1972.

Sheffey, Ruthe T. and Eugenia Collier. Impressions in the
Asphalt Jungle of Urban America in Literature. New
York: Scribner, 1972.

SHORT STORIES

"Marigold," Black World 19:1 (November 1969), 54-62.

"Sinbad the Cat," Black World 20:9 (July 1971), 53-55.

"Sweet Potato Pie," Black World 21:10 (August 1972), 54-62.

CRITICISM AND REVIEWS

"Afro-American Writers," Black World 19:11 (September 1970),
92-93.

"Ain't Supposed to Die a Natural Death," Black World 21:6
(April 1972), 79-81.

"Black Phoenix," Black World 19:11 (September 1970), 77.

"The Endless Journey of an Ex-Colored Man," Phylon 32
(Fourth Quarter, Winter 1971), 365-373.

"The Four-Way Dilemma of Claude McKay," CLA Journal 15
(March 1972), 345-353.

"Heritage from Harlem," Black World 20:1 (November 1970),
52-59.

"I Do Not Marvel, Countee Cullen," CLA Journal 11 (1967), 73-87.

"James Weldon Johnson: Mirror of Change," Phylon 21 (1960), 351-359.

"The Nightmare Truth of an Invisible Man," Black World 20:2 (December 1970), 12-19.

"A Pain in His Soul: Simple as Epic Hero." In Langston Hughes: Black Genius, ed. by Therman O'Daniel. New York: William Morrow, 1971.

"The Phrase Unbearably Repeated," Phylon 25 (1964), 288-296.

"Some Black and Fettered Women," Black World 21:1 (November 1971), 41.

"Thematic Patterns in Baldwin's Essays," Black World 21:8 (June, 1972), 28-34.

SHIRLEY GRAHAM DUBOIS
(also just Shirley Graham)

BOOKS

Booker T. Washington. New York: Messner, 1955.

George Washington Carver. New York: Messner, 1944.

His Day Is Marching On: A Memoir of W. E. B. DuBois. Philadelphia: J. B. Lippincott, 1971.

John Baptiste DuSable. New York: Messner, 1953.

The Story of Paul Robeson. New York: Julian Messner, 1967.

The Story of Phillis Wheatley: Poetess of the American Revolution. New York: Messner, 1949.

There Was Once a Slave: The Heroic Story of Frederick Douglass. New York: Julian Messner, 1966.

Your Most Humble Servant: The Story of Benjamin Banneker.
New York: Messner, 1949.

Zulu Heart. New York: Joseph Opaku Publishing Co., 1974.

ARTICLES

"After Addis Ababa: A Report on the African Summit Conference," Freedomways 3 (Fall 1963), 471-485.

"Egypt Is Africa," Pt. 1. The Black Scholar 1 (May 1970),
20-22.

"Egypt Is Africa," Pt. 2. The Black Scholar 2 (September
1970), 28-34.

"The Liberation of Africa," The Black Scholar 2 (February
1971), 32-37.

"Nation Building in Ghana," Freedomways 2 (Fall 1962), 371-
376.

"Negroes in the American Revolution," Freedomways (Summer
1961).

"[Review:] Africa Must Unite, by Kwame Nkrumah," Freedomways 3:1 (Fall 1963), 562-566.

"Spirituals to Symphonies," Etude 54 (November 1936), 691.

"The Struggle in Lesotho," The Black Scholar 2 (November
1970), 25-29.

"Tribute to Paul Robeson," Freedomways 11:1 (First Quarter,
1971), 6-7.

PLAYS

Cool Dust, Karamu Theatre. (Unpublished).

Elijah's Ravens, Karamu Theatre. (Unpublished).

It's Morning. (Unpublished).

Track Thirteen. Boston: Expression Co., 1940.

MUSICAL COMPOSITIONS

Little Black Sambo, 1938. (Unpublished.)

Tom-Tom, 1932. Three-act opera premiered in concert form
    by NBC Radio June 26, 1932. Stage performance, Cleve-
    land Stadium, 1932.

JESSIE FAUSET

BOOKS

The Chinaberry Tree. New York: Frederick A. Stokes Co.,
    1931; repr. 1961.

Comedy, American Style. New York: Frederick A. Stokes,
    1933; repr. 1969.

Plum Bun. New York: Frederick A. Stokes, 1929.

There Is Confusion. New York: Boni and Liveright, 1924.

ARTICLES

"The Gift of Laughter." In Black Expression, ed. by Ad-
    dison Gayle. New York: Weybright and Talley, 1969.

STORIES

"The Meal." In Afro-American Voices, 1700s-1970s. Los
    Angeles: Oxford Book Co., 1970.

BIOGRAPHY AND CRITICISM

Adams, Russell L. Great Negroes Past and Present. Chica-
    go: Afro-Am Pub. Co., 1963, p. 117.

Bone, Robert. "The Rear Guard." In The Negro Novel in
    America. New Haven, Conn.: Yale University Press,
    1968.

Brawley, Benjamin. "Protest and Vindication." In The
Negro Genius. New York: Dodd, Mead, 1937.

Williams, Kenny Jackson. They Also Spoke. Nashville:
Townsend Press, 1970.

NIKKI GIOVANNI

BOOKS

Black Feeling, Black Talk, Black Judgment. New York:
William Morrow, 1968.

My House. New York: William Morrow, 1972.

Night Comes Softly [editor]. New York: Nik-Tom Publications, 1970.

Spin a Soft Black Song: Poems for Children. New York:
Hill and Wang, 1971.

AUTOBIOGRAPHY

Gemini: An Extended Autobiographical Statement. Indianapolis: Bobbs-Merrill, 1971.

ARTICLES

"Black Poems, Poseurs, and Power," Negro Digest 18:8 (June
1969), 30-34.

"The Planet of Junior Brown," Black World 21:6 (March 1972),
70-71.

AUDIO-VISUALS

Truth Is on Its Way. Right-on Recording.

BIOGRAPHY AND CRITICISM

Bailey, Peter. "Nikki Giovanni: 'I Am Black, Female,

Polite,'" Ebony 27 (February 1972), 48-52, 53-54, 56.

Brooks, Russell. "The Motifs of Dynamic Change in Black
Revolutionary Poetry," CLA Journal 15 (September
1972), 7-17.

Lee, Don L. "The Poets and Their Poetry: There Is a Tra-
dition." In Dynamite Voices: Black Poets of the 1960s.
Detroit: Broadside Press, 1971, pp. 68-74.

Palmer, R. Roderick. "The Poetry of Three Revolutionists:
Don L. Lee, Sonia Sanchez, and Nikki Giovanni," CLA
Journal 15 (September 1971), 25-36.

LORRAINE HANSBERRY

BOOKS

Les Blancs: The Collected Last Plays of Lorraine Hansberry
["Les Blancs," "The Drinking Gourd," "What Use Are
the Flowers?"], ed. with critical backgrounds by Robert
Nemiroff, and with an intro. by Julius Lester. New
York: Random House, 1972.

The Movement: Documentary of a Struggle for Equality. New
York: Simon and Schuster, 1964.

A Raisin in the Sun. New York: Random House, 1959 (A
Signet Book, 1961).

The Sign in Sidney Brustein's Window. Intro. by Robert Nemiroff, Foreward by John Baine. New York: Random
House, 1965 (A Signet Book, 1966).

To Be Young, Gifted and Black: A Portrait of Lorraine Hansberry in Her Own Words [play]. Adapted by Robert
Nemiroff. New York: Samuel French, 1971.

To Be Young, Gifted and Black: Lorraine Hansberry in Her
Own Words [autobiography]. Adapted by Robert Nemi-
roff with an intro. by James Baldwin. Englewood
Cliffs, N.J.: Prentice-Hall, 1969.

POEMS

"Flag from a Kitchenette Window," Masses and Mainstream
    3 (September 1950), 38-40.

"For a Young Negro I Have Met, A Love Song," To Be Young,
    Gifted and Black, pp. 80-81.

"Interim," To Be Young, Gifted and Black, p. 90.

"Lynchsong," Masses and Mainstream 4 (July 1951), 19-20.

ARTICLES AND SPEECHES

"The Black Revolution and the White Backlash" [transcript of
    a Town Hall forum with Ossie Davis, Ruby Dee, Lor-
    raine Hansberry, Leroi Jones, John O. Killens, Paule
    Marshall, Charles E. Silberman, James Wechsler, and
    David Susskind, moderator]. Almost complete trans-
    cript: National Guardian 26 (July 4, 1964), 5-9. Par-
    tial excerpts: Black Protest, ed. with an intro. and
    commentaries by Joanne Grant. New York: Fawcett
    World Library, 1968.

"A Challenge to Artists." (Speech advocating the abolition of
    the House UnAmerican Activities Committee.) Free-
    domways 3 (Winter 1963), 33-35. Reprinted in Harlem
    USA, ed. by John Henrik Clarke. Berlin: Seven Seas
    Books, 1964.

"Congolese Patriot" [letter to the editor]. The New York
    Times Magazine, March 26, 1961, p. 4.

"The Creative Use of the Unconscious," "Annals of Psycho-
    therapy," Journal of the American Academy of Psycho-
    therapists 5 (1964), 13-17.

"Genet, Mailer and the New Paternalism," Village Voice,
    June 1, 1961, pp. 10-15.

"Images and Essences: 1961 Dialogue with an Uncolored Egg-
    head Containing Wholesome Intentions and Some Sass,"
    The Urbanite 1 (May 1961), 10, 11, 36. (Dramatized
    version in To Be Young, Gifted and Black.)

"The Legacy of W. E. B. DuBois." In Black Titan:

W. E. B. DeBois, ed. by John Henrik Clarke, Ester
Jackson, Ernest Kaiser, J. H. Odell. Boston: Beacon
Press, 1970.

"A Letter from Lorraine Hansberry on Porgy and Bess,"
The Theater, August 1959, p. 10.

"Me Tink Me Hear Sounds in De Night," Theatre Arts 44
(October 1964), 9-11, 69-70. Reprinted as "The Negro
in the American Theater" in American Playwrights on
Drama, ed. by Horst Frenz. New York: Hill and Wang,
1965.

"Miss Hansberry on 'Backlash,'" Village Voice, July 23,
1964, pp. 10, 16.

"My Name Is Lorraine Hansberry, I Am a Writer," Esquire
72 (November 1969), 140.

"The Nation Needs Your Gifts," Negro Digest 13:10 (August
1964), 26-29.

"The Negro in American Culture" [symposium with James
Baldwin, Emile Capouya, Lorraine Hansberry, Nat Hen-
toff, Langston Hughes, and Alfred Kazin]. Reprinted
in The Black American Writer, Vol. I: Fiction, ed.
by C. W. E. Bigsby. Baltimore: Pelican Books, 1971.

"Negroes and Africa." Quoted extensively in this chapter in
The New World of Negro Americans, ed. by Harold
R. Isaacs. New York: John Day Co., 1965.

BIOGRAPHY AND CRITICISM

Abramson, Doris E. Negro Playwrights in the American
Theatre, 1925-1959. New York: Columbia University
Press, 1969.

Isaacs, Harold. "Five Writers and Their African Ancestors:
Part I," Phylon 21 (1960), 66-70.

Killens, John O. "Broadway in Black and White," A Forum
I:iii (1965), 66-70.

"Les Blancs," Nation 211 (November 30, 1970), 573.

Lewis, Theophilus. "Social Protest in A Raisin in the Sun,"
Catholic World 190 (1959), 31-35.

Mitchell, Loften. Black Drama. New York: Hawthorn
Books, 1967.

"The Sign in Sidney Brustein's Window," National Review 17
(March 23, 1965), 250.

To Be Young, Gifted and Black [autobiography and collection
of separate writings]. Adapted by Robert Nemiroff with
an intro. by James Baldwin. Englewood Cliffs, N.J.:
Prentice-Hall, 1969. (Signet Book--New American Library, 1970).

AUDIO-VISUALS

Lorraine Hansberry Speaks Out: Art and the Black Revolution.
Selected and ed. by Robert Nemiroff. New York: Caedmon Records, 1972.

A Raisin in the Sun. (The complete play, 3 records with Ossie Davis, Ruby Dee, Claudia McNeil, Diana Sands,
Leonard Jackson, Zakes Mokae, Sam Schacht, Harold
Scott.) Directed by Lloyd Richards. New York: Caedmon Records, 1972.

To Be Young, Gifted and Black. (The complete play, 3 re-
cords with James Earl Jones, Barbara Baxley, Claudia
McNeil, Tina Sattin, Camille Yarbrough, Garn Stevens,
John Towey.) Directed by Gigi Cascio and Robert
Nemiroff. New York: Caedmon Records, 1971.

ZORA NEALE HURSTON

BOOKS

Dust Tracks on a Road. Philadelphia: J. B. Lippincott,
1942.

Jonah's Gourd Vine. Philadelphia: J. B. Lippincott, 1934.

Moses, Man of the Mountain. Philadelphia: J. B. Lippincott, 1935.

Mules and Men. Philadelphia: J. B. Lippincott, 1938.

Seraph on the Suwanee. New York: Charles Scribner's Sons,
    1948.

Tell My Horse. Philadelphia: J. B. Lippincott, 1938.

Their Eyes Were Watching God. Philadelphia: J. B. Lippin-
    cott, 1937.

ARTICLES

"I Saw Negro Votes Peddled," American Legion Magazine,
    November 1950, pp. 12-13, 45-57, 59-60.

"A Negro Voter Sizes Up Taft," The Saturday Evening Post
    244 (December 8, 1951), 29, 150-152.

"What White Publishers Won't Print," Negro Digest 5:6 (April
    1947), 85-89.

STORIES

"Drenched in Light," Opportunity 2 (December 1924), 371-374.

"The Gilded Six-Bits." In Story in America, ed. by Whit
    Burnett and Martha Foley. New York: Vanguard, 1934.

"John Redding Goes to Sea," Opportunity 4 (January 1926),
    16-21.

"Spunk," Opportunity 3 (May 1925), 171-173.

"Sweat." In Black American Literature: Essays, Poetry,
    Fiction, Drama, ed. by Darwin T. Turner. Columbus,
    Ohio: Merrill, 1970.

PLAYS

"The First One, a Play." In Ebony and Topaz, a Collec-
    tanea, ed. by Charles S. Johnson. New York: National
    Urban League, 1927.

"Mulebone: A Comedy of Negro Life in Three Acts," by
    Langston Hughes and Zora Neale Hurston. New York,

1931 (Unpublished).

"Polk County, A Comedy of Negro Life on a Sawmill Camp."
(Unpublished.)

OTHER UNPUBLISHED WORKS

"Book of Harlem."

"The Emperor Effaces Himself in Harlem Language."

BIOGRAPHY AND CRITICISM

Blake, E. L. "Zora Neale Hurston: Author and Folklorist,"
Negro History Bulletin 29 (April 1966), 149-150.

Byrd, James W. "Zora Neale Hurston: A Novel Folklorist,"
Tennessee Folklore Society Bulletin 20 (1955), 37-41.

Hughes, Langston. "Black Renaissance." In The Big Sea.
New York: Knopf, 1940.

Hurst, Fannie. "Zora Hurston: A Personality Sketch," Yale
University Library Gazette 35 (1961), 17-22.

Jackson, Blyden. "Some Negroes in the Land of Goshen."
Tennessee Folklore Society Bulletin 19 (1953), 103-107.

Pratt, Theodore. "A Memoir: Zora Neale Hurston, Florida's
First Distinguished Author," Negro Digest (February
1962), 52-56.

Turner, Darwin T. "The Negro Novelist and the South,"
Southern Humanities Review 1 (1967), 21-29.

_____. "Zora Neale Hurston: The Wandering Minstrel,"
In In a Minor Chord: Three Afro-American Writers
and Their Search for Identity. Carbondale, Ill. :
Southern Illinois University Press, 1971.

NAOMI LONG MADGETT

BOOKS (Poems)

One and the Many. New York: Exposition, 1956.

Pink Ladies in the Afternoon. Detroit: Lotus Press, 1972.

Star by Star. Detroit: Harlo, 1963.

Songs to a Phantom Nightingale. New York: Fortuny's, 1941.

SINGLE POEMS

"Black Woman." Copyright 1970 by Naomi Long Madgett.

"Sunny." Detroit: Broadside Series.

AUDIO-VISUALS (Video Tapes)

Naomi Madgett, Donald Hall, and Dan Gerber Reading Their
    Poems and Talking to Students. Michigan Council for
    the Arts, 10125 E. Jefferson Ave., Detroit, Michigan
    48214.

Poets Reading Their Poetry for OCC-TV. Robert Hayden,
    Naomi Madgett, and Dudley Randall Read the Six Poems
    They Want To Be Remembered By. 8mm. Black and
    white. 50 min. Rental: Oakland Community College,
    Orchard Lake, Michigan 48030.

ANN PETRY

BOOKS

Country Place. Boston: Houghton Mifflin, 1947.

Harriet Tubman: Conductor of the Underground Railway. New
    York: Crowell, 1955.

Legends of the Saints. New York: Crowell, 1972.

Ann Petry

"Miss Muriel" and Other Stories.   Boston: Houghton Mifflin,
     1971.

The Narrows.   Boston: Houghton Mifflin, 1953.

The Street.   Boston: Houghton Mifflin, 1946.

Tituba of Salem Village.   New York: Thomas Y. Crowell, 1964.

STORIES

"Harlem," Holiday (April 1949).

"In Darkness and Confusion." In Black Voices, ed. by
   Abraham Chapman. New York: Mentor Books, 1968.

"Like a Winding Sheet." In The Best American Short
   Stories, 1946.

BIOGRAPHY AND CRITICISM

Bone, Robert. The Negro Novel in America. New Haven,
   Conn.: Yale University Press, 1968, pp. 180-185.

Dempsey, David. "Uncle Tom's Ghost and the Literary Abolitionist," Antioch Review 6 (1946), 442-448.

Green, Marjorie. "Ann Petry Planned to Write," Opportunity: A Journal of Negro Life 24 (1946), 78-79.

Ivy, James. "Ann Petry Talks About Her First Novel,"
   The Crisis 53 (1946), 48-49.

_____. "Mrs. Petry's Harlem," The Crisis 53 (1946),
   43-46.

Littlejohn, David. Black on White: A Critical Survey of
   Writing by American Negroes. New York: Viking
   Press, 1966, pp. 154-156.

Maund, Alfred. "The Negro Novelist and the Contemporary
   American Scene," Chicago Jewish Forum 12 (1954),
   28-34.

"On an Author," New York Herald Tribune, August 16, 1953,
   p. 3.

Richardson, Ben. Great American Negroes. New York:
   Thomas Y. Crowell, 1956.

DOROTHY PORTER

BOOKS

Early Negro Writing 1760-1840. Boston: Beacon Press, 1970. (Collection of Black history, literature, music at Howard University.)

North American Negro Poets: A Bibliographical Check List of Their Writings, 1760-1944. Hattiesburg, Miss. : The Book Farm, 1945.

A Selected List of Books By and about the Negro. Washington, D. C. , 1936.

A Working Bibliography of the Negro in the United States. Ann Arbor, Mich. : University Microfilms, 1969.

ARTICLES

"The African Collection at Howard University," African Studies Bulletin 2 (January 1959), 17-21.

"David Ruggles, 1810-1849: Hydropathic Practitioner," Journal of the National Medical Association 49 (January 1957), 67-72, and (March 1957), 130-134.

"Glimpse of Negro History," Negro History Bulletin 16 (April 1953), 146, 164-165.

"Maria Louise Baldwin," Journal of Negro Education 21 (Winter 1952), 92-96.

"The Organized Educational Activities of Negro Literary Societies, 1818-1846," Journal of Negro Education (1936).

"Sarah Parker Redmond," Journal of Negro History 20 (April 1935), 287-293.

"Some Recent Literature Pertaining to the American Negro," Wilson Library Bulletin 9 (June 1935), 569-570.

Porter, Dorothy and Ethel M. Ellis. "Index to the Journal of Negro Life and History," Journal of Negro Education 5 (April 1936), 232-244.

SONIA SANCHEZ

BOOKS

Homecoming. Detroit: Broadside Press, 1968.

It's a New Day. Detroit: Broadside Press, 1971.

We a BadddDDD People. Detroit: Broadside Press, 1970.

PLAYS

"Sister Son/Ji." In New Plays from the Black Theatre,
    ed. and with an intro. by Bullins. New York: Ban-
    tam Books, 1969.

SINGLE POEMS

"For Our Lady." In Natural Process, ed. by Ted Wilentz
    and Tom Weatherly. New York: Hill and Wang, 1970.

Liberation Poem. Detroit: Broadside Press, 1971.

"Malcolm." In For Malcolm, ed. by Dudley Randall and
    Margaret G. Burroughs. Detroit: Broadside Press,
    1967.

"right-on: white America." In Soulscript: Afro-American
    Poetry, ed. by June Jordan. New York: Doubleday,
    1970.

AUDIO-VISUALS

Homecoming. Broadside Voices. 5-inch reel, $5.00.

We a BadddDDD People. Broadside Voices. 5-inch reel,
    $5.00.

BIOGRAPHY AND CRITICISM

Brooks, A Russell. "The Motif of Dynamic Change in Black
    Revolutionary Poetry," CLA Journal 15 (September 1971),
    25-36.

Clarke, Sebastian. "Sonia Sanchez and Her Work," Black
    World 20 (June 1971), 45-48, 96-98.

Lee, Donald L. "The Poets and Their Poetry." In Dynamite
    Voices I: Black Poets of the 1960's, ed. by Don L. Lee.
    Detroit: Broadside Press, 1971.

PHILIPPA DUKE SCHUYLER

BOOKS

Adventure in Black and White. New York: P. Speller, 1960.

Good Men Die. Denver, Colo.: Twin Circle, 1969.

Jungle Saints. New York: Herder and Herder, 1963.

Who Killed the Congo? New York: Devin-Adair, 1962.

[With Josephine Schuyler]. Kingdom of Dreams. New York:
    P. Speller, 1966.

POEM

"A Baby on Death," Washington Post, May 10, 1967.

ARTICLES

"Meet the George Schuyler's," Our World 6 (April 1951), 22-
    26.

"Music of Modern Africa," Music Journal 18 (October 1960),
    18, 60-63.

"Why I Don't Marry," Ebony 13 (July 1958), 78-80.

(SOME) MUSICAL COMPOSITIONS

African Rhapsody. Philippa Duke Schuyler, copyright, 1965.

Around the World Suite. Philippa Duke Schuyler, 1960.

Chisamharu the Nogomo (Mozambique).   Premiered at New
    York Town Hall, Sunday, September 13, 1964.

Country Boy.   Arr. by Juan Hines and Philippa Schuyler,
    copyright 1957.

Cynthia. Juan Hines. Arr. by Juan Hines and Philippa
    Schuyler, copyright 1957.

Eight Little Pieces.   For piano.

The Legend of the Mahdi.   Based on themes from Omdurman,
    Sudan. Music copyright by Philippa Duke Schuyler, 1965.

Manhattan Nocturne.   Scored by Miss Schuyler for 100-piece
    symphony, 1943.   Premiered by the New York Philhar-
    monic Orchestra at Carnegie Hall.   First-prize com-
    position in Grinnell Foundation Contest, Detroit.   Also
    performed by the Chicago and San Francisco Symphonies.

New Moon.   Arr. by Philippa Schuyler and John Kelly.   Copy-
    right, 1960.

The Nile Fantasy.   1. "Inshallah, or Fate ... Contemplation
    and Submission"; 2. "Violence and Terror"; 3. "The
    Long Road to Peace." For piano and orchestra.   Pre-
    miered in Cairo, Egypt, by the Cairo Symphony Orches-
    tra with Miss Schuyler as soloist, December 10, 1965.
    Premiered in America at a memorial recital for Miss
    Schuyler, September 24, 1967, Leonard de Paur, con-
    ductor.   Margaret Bonds, arranger.

No Bed of Roses.   Words and music by Juan Hines.   Arr.
    by Philippa Duke Schuyler.   1957.

Old Father William; Arabian Love Song; Hymn to Proserpina;
    and Maelstrom; ca. 1948.

The Rhapsody of Youth, 1948.   Premiered in Port au Prince,
    Haiti, 1948.   Miss Schuyler received the Medal of Me-
    rit and Honor from President Paul E. Magloire for this
    composition.

Rococo.   Words by Charles A. Swinburne.   Words and music,
    Philippa Duke Schuyler.   New words changed and added.
    Philippa Duke Schuyler, 1961.

Rumpelstiltskin. Scherzo from her Fairytale Symphony.
Scored by Miss Schuyler, 1943. Premiered by the New
York Philharmonic Orchestra, 1944. Also played by
the Boston Pops and Cincinnati Symphony. 50 pp.

Rumpelstiltsken. para piano, musica y arrangement de Philippa Duke Schuyler. Buenos Aires, Ricordi Americana.
12 pp.

Sleepy Hollow Sketches, 1946. The piano transcription was
premiered at a United Nations celebration, Tarrytown
on the Hudson, birthplace of Washington Irving.

Three Little Pieces. Copyright Mrs. George Schuyler, November 10, 1938.

Three Songs. Sung as part of the Philippa Schuyler Memorial
Concert, by Camilla Williams, September 24, 1967, New
York Town Hall. Leonard De Paur, conductor.

The White Nile Suite. Piano solo (musical saga depicting
Arab history in Egypt and the Sudan). Philippa Duke
Schuyler, 1965.

"The Wolf," "Autumn Rain," "The Jolly Pig." Three Little
Pieces. For piano, 1938.

BIOGRAPHY AND CRITICISM

"Back from Latin American Tour," Musical Courier 147
(April 15, 1953), 24.

"Buenos Aires Series Re-Engages Pianist," Musical America
75 (February 1, 1955), 14.

Cummings, Robert. "Allegorically Speaking," Music Journal
25 (November 9, 1967), 4.

Ferguson, C. W. "Americans Not Everybody Knows," PTA
Magazine 62 (May 30, 1967), 12-14.

"Harlem Prodigy," Time 27 (June 22, 1936), 40.

"The International Scene," Musical Courier 159 (April 1959),
18.

"Music by Philippa," Newsweek 28 (August 14, 1944), 84.

" 'Original Girl' Wins Prizes in Grinnell Foundation Contest," Time 47 (March 25, 1946), 62.

"Philippa Duke Schuyler," Crisis 57 (May 1950), 276-333, 334.

"Philippa Duke Schuyler," Crisis 61 (April 1954), 207.

"Philippa Duke Schuyler," Crisis 74 (June 1967), 248.

"Philippa Duke Schuyler," Musical America 76 (November 15, 1956), 20. (Town Hall Recital).

"Philippa Duke Schuyler," Musical Courier 149 (May 15, 1954), 28.

"Philippa Duke Schuyler," Musical Courier 150 (October 1954), 30.

"Philippa Duke Schuyler," Musical Courier, 1959. Directory of the Musical Arts and Artists, p. 181.

"Philippa Duke Schuyler," Revue Musica Chilena 10 (January 1955), 77.

"Philippa Duke Schuyler Back from Europe," Musical Courier 149 (January 1, 1954), 20.

"Philippa Schuyler: American Pianist Played for Monarchs and Desert Saint," Musical Courier 159 (May, 1959), 12.

"Philippa Schuyler Makes Orchestral Debut in Buenos Aires." From Porteno Press on Philippa's Argentina Debut. Reprinted in Crisis 61 (December 1954), 600-602.

Schuyler, Josephine. "My Daughter Philippa," Sepia 7 (May 1959), 8-12.

_____. "Race, Diet and Intelligence," Crisis 76 (May 1969), 207-210.

U. S. Pianist Killed in Vietnam Crash," New York Times, Wednesday, May 10, 1967, pp. 1, 5.

"Up and Down the Guild Keyboard," Musical Courier 153 (January 1, 1956), 2.

AUDIO-VISUALS

International Favorites: Philippa Schuyler, Pianist. Mono
    Vol. I, Middle Tone Records, New York: Emanuel A.
    Middleton Music Pub. [1576 Broadway, N. Y. 10036].

ALICE WALKER (Mrs. Mal Levanthal, 1944)

BOOKS

Once: Poems. New York: Harcourt, 1968.

Petunias. Volume of poetry. Forthcoming from Harcourt,
    Brace, Jovanovich.

Textual Problems of the First Folio. Philadelphia: R. West,
    1973; repr. of 1953 ed.

The Third Life of Grange Copeland. New York: Harcourt,
    1970.

SHORT STORIES

"Diary of an African Nun." In The Black Women, ed. by Toni
    Cade. New York, 1970.

"Roselly," MS. 1 (August 1972), 44-47.

"To Hell with Dying." In Best Short Stories by Negro Writers,
    ed. by Langston Hughes. Boston: Little, Brown and
    Co. , 1967.

"The Welcome Table," Freedomways 10 (Third Quarter 1970),
    242-246.

POEMS

"Facing the Way," and "Forgiveness," Freedomways 15
    (Fourth Quarter, 1975), 265-267.

"Hymn." In Afro-American Literature: An Introduction, ed.
    by Robert Hayden and others. New York: Harcourt,
    Brace, Jovanovich, Inc. , 1971.

"In These Dissenting Times: I, The Old Men Used to Sing;
II, Winking at a Funeral; III, Women; IV, Three Dol-
lars Cash; V, You Had to Go to Funerals," Black World
20:1 (November 1970), 60-83.

"Rock Eagle," and "South," Freedomways 2 (Fourth Quarter
1971), 367.

"Talking to My Grandmother Who Died Poor Some Years Ago
(While Listening to Richard Nixon Declare, 'I Am Not
a Crook')," Black Scholar 9:6 (June, 1975), 62.

"Thief," and "Gift," Essence 3 (July 1972), 60.

ARTICLES

"Beyond the Peacock: The Reconstruction of Flannery O'Con-
ner," Ms. 4:4 (December 1975), 77-79, 102-106.

"A Daring Subject Boldly Shared." Review of Loving Her, by
Ann Shockley. Indianapolis: Bobbs-Merrill, 1976. In
Ms. 3:10 (April 1976), 120-124.

"In Search of Zora Neale Hurston," Ms. 3 (March, 1975),
74-79.

Untitled review of Good Morning Revolution: Uncollected
Writings of Social Protest by Langston Hughes, ed. by
Faith Berry; foreword by Saunders Redding. New York:
Hill and Co. In The Black Scholar 7:10 (July-August
1976), 53-55.

"A Writer Because of, Not in Spite of, Her Children." Review of Second Class Citizen, by Buchi Emecheta. In
Ms. 2, 4 (January, 1976), 106.

BIOGRAPHY AND CRITICISM

Fowler, Carolyn. "Solid at the Core." A review of In Love
and Trouble: Stories of Black Women, by Alice Walker.
New York: Harcourt, Brace, Jovanovich, 1973. In
Freedomways 14 (First Quarter 1974), 59-62.

Kuel, Linda. "Takes Two." Review of Sula, by Toni Morrison and In Love and Trouble, by Alice Walker. In
Viva 1:6 (March, 1974), 35.

Rogers, Norma. "Struggle for Humanity." Review of Meri-
    dian, by Alice Walker. New York: Harcourt, Brace,
    Jovanovich, 1976. In Freedomways 16 (Second Quarter,
    1976), 120-122.

Trescott, Jacqueline. "The Friction of Paradoxes Sparkles
    with Alice Walker," Washington Post, Sunday, Septem-
    ber 19, 1976, p. 26.

MARGARET WALKER

BOOKS

For My People. New Haven, Conn.: Yale University Press,
    1942.

How I Wrote Jubilee. Chicago: Third World Press, 1972.

Jubilee. Boston: Houghton, Mifflin, 1966. (Novel)

October Journey. Detroit: Broadside, 1973.

Prophets for a New Day. Detroit: Broadside, 1970.

ARTICLES

"Nausea of Sartre," Yale Review 42 (December 1952), 251-
    271.

"New Poets." In Black Expression, ed. by Addison Gayle,
    Jr. New York: Weybright and Talley, 1969.

AUDIO-VISUALS

"For My People," "Old Molly Means," "Kissie Lee," "Stacka-
    lee," and "John Henry." Anthology of Negro Poets,
    Folkway Records FL 9791.

Prophets for a New Day. Detroit: Broadside, $5.00 (tape).

BIOGRAPHY AND CRITICISM

Current Biography (1943).

Emanuel, James and Theodore Cross, eds. Dark Symphony. New York: Free Press, 1968, pp. 493, 494.

Giddings, Paula. "A Shoulder Hunched Against a Sharp Concern: Some Themes in the Poetry of Margaret Walker," Black World 21:2 (December 1971), 20-25.

Littlejohn, David. Black on White: A Critical Survey of Writing by American Negroes. New York: Viking Press, 1966.

Randall, Dudley. "The Black Aesthetics in the Thirties, Forties, and Fifties." In The Black Aesthetic, ed. by Addison Gayle, Jr. New York: Doubleday, 1971.

Rollins, Charlemae. Famous American Poets. New York: Dodd, Mead, 1965.

IDEAS AND ACHIEVEMENTS
OF SOME AMERICAN BLACK WOMEN

This listing of significant ideas and achievements of American Black women is a challenging one for the stimulating information that it provides. It is by necessity an extremely limited list, including the ideas of only forty women, because of this researcher's lack of funds. The women whose ideas are presented here are from the past and present and are from all walks of life.

ANGELOU, MAYA (author, civil rights worker, dancer, lecturer, performer) became the first Black woman to create a movie screenplay when she produced Georgia, Georgia.

BAKER, ELLA (civil activist) has been described as "undoubtedly one of the great Black female figures of all times." Mrs. Baker is credited with organizing SCLC; is called the "mother of SNCC"; and was an important field worker for the NAACP, building chapters throughout the South.

BAKER, JOSEPHINE (1907-1975), star of the Folies Bèrgere during the '20s and '30s, legally adopted 12 children from various races to prove that people of all races and colors can live together harmoniously.

BARRETT, JANIE PORTER (first superintendent of the Virginia Industrial Home for Colored Girls) organized the Locust Street Social Settlement in her Hampton home so that young boys and girls could be kept off the streets. Through a variety of activities, young people learned "thrift, happiness, and healthy social contact." As superintendent of the Industrial Home, Mrs. Barrett employed new methods for rehabilitation. Girls were made to feel that they were beginning life anew at the home and that they could become the best women in the world. Mrs. Barrett considered the home to be a "moral hospital where each girl is studied and given individual treatment" with the intention of rehabilitation and building character.

BETHUNE, MARY McLEOD, was another Black woman who had many dreams which she carried out admirably. She wanted to start a school for youth. With $1.50 she started a school on what had been a dump. The school is now Bethune Cookman College, Daytona, Florida. Because there was not one hospital within two hundred miles on the Atlantic Coast where Blacks could receive medical treatment, she started an infirmary which grew into a hospital and training school for nurses. In her last will and testament Mary McLeod Bethune left part of her dream to succeeding generations: Love; Hope; Confidence in one another; Respect for the uses of power intelligently directed; Faith; Racial dignity; a Desire to live harmoniously with other men.

BOWEN, UVELIA (Organizer, social-service worker, teacher) has created, with the help of her family and friends in Philadelphia, a personal resources agency which has as its purpose giving everyone an equal opportunity and letting the integrity and ability of the individual decide the choice of occupation and position in life.

BURROUGHS, NANNIE (educator, author, organizer, lecturer) organized the Harriet Beecher Literary Society as a vehicle for literary expression; organized the Woman's Industrial Club, which provided low priced and wholesome meals to a "select group of office people"; fostered the idea of a national training school for girls in need of help. The school, opened in 1907, was called the three "B's": the Bible, the Bath, and the Broom, representing "clean lives, clean bodies, and clean homes." In her early endeavors, Miss Burroughs insisted that people valued that for which they paid. (Women Builders, Sadie Iola Daniels.)

CHAMBERLAIN, NAOMI (educator) has developed a series of innovative health religious education programs. One series, which is based on scriptures from the Bible, is called the "Reach Out and Touch Program." This particular program has a religious format and includes a mass which Miss Chamberlain wrote about lead poisoning.

CHISHOLM, SHIRLEY (politician and first Black woman to sit in Congress) decided that she had the qualifications to run for the highest office in the land. She did; and although unsuccessful in her bid to win the Democratic nomination, inspired many women with the idea that a woman could run and possibly become president of the United States.

CLAYTON, MAYME (historian and collector of rare books by black authors) has realized her dream of becoming a rare-book dealer in Los Angeles. Mrs. Clayton has collected more than 3,000 first edition books about Black history and literature, most of which were published before the twentieth century.

COLEMAN, BEVERLY (director of a preventive health center in North Hollywood, poet, teacher) founded a health center called Natches for the general purpose of effecting a preventive approach to health care. Her activities attempt to validate Afro-Asiatic ideas as models to prevent diseases and synthesize the arts of healthful living.

COLTRANE, ALICE (Turiya Aparna--Widow of John Coltrane--harpist, organist, pianist) is also a Jazz luminary who combines African and Asian mysticism with Western sounds.

COPPIN, FANNIE (educator trained in Latin, Greek, and mathematics) believed in the training of hand and mind, a theory she executed at the Institute for Colored Youth, Philadelphia, after becoming principal of that school in 1866. She organized a home for girls and young women, and the Colored Women's Exchange; wrote a new constitution for the 1892 General Conference of the A. M. E. Church; and decreed that methods of instruction should include certain philosophies. The word "dumb" should never be used in a classroom; a child's lunch should never be taken from him, for there is no use in trying to teach a hungry child; improper ventilation of a room often contributes to sluggish children; teachers should always remember that they are dealing with a human being, whose needs are like the teacher's. She maintained that reading and writing should be taught through sentences; and that writing should be taught through letter writing.

DELTA SIGMA THETA SORORITY decided to counteract the Black exploitation films of the 1970s with a positive film, Count Down at Kusini.

DERRICOTE, TOI coordinated a first for Rutgers University when she arranged the University's first Black Poetry Festival, April, 1977.

EVANS, DONNA and BARBARA WILKINS (teacher and dancer,

respectively) dreamed of a school, now the Children's Union, Inc., in Long Beach, Ca., that would prepare disadvantaged children to survive and progress in a technological society.

FORTEN, CHARLOTTE (abolitionist, author, educator) was one of the first individuals to analyze the Negro spirituals that she heard while teaching during the Civil War in the Sea Islands of South Carolina.

HACKLEY, E. AZALIA, for whom a collection in the Detroit Public Library has been named, traveled throughout the United States holding folksong festivals through which she taught Black communities to sing and appreciate Negro folksongs. Miss Hackley, who had been a concert singer, had a music store and publishing house in Chicago in 1918. At that time she encouraged the Black community to give Black compositions as Christmas presents or to rent their musical instruments from her store.

HAMER, FANNIE LOU (devoted civil rights worker, former field secretary for SNCC, politician) helped to organize the Mississippi Freedom Democratic Party and was one of its spokesmen at the Democratic Convention in 1964. At this time the newly-formed party challenged the legality of the all-White Mississippi delegation. Later, she was one of three Black candidates to run for Congress. On one occasion when she had been jailed for her civil rights activities, she was stripped to the waist, held by a Black man, and beaten by White men until she bled profusely. It was at that time that Mrs. Hamer came to understand that the Black man must be praised and reinforced to neutralize the dehumanization he experiences from White America.

HANDY, D. ANTOINETTE (author, concert flutist, educator, flute clinician, lecturer) organized and manages the Trio Pro Viva, an American-based group that has toured the Southern college circuit. Miss Handy performs and is constantly looking for compositions by contemporary Black composers.

HEWETT, MARY JANE (author, lecturer, educator) is examining the Black experience in the New World through the prism of Black women because she sees women as culture bearers. Mrs. Hewett is using Louise Bennett of the West Indies and Zora N. Hurston as her prime subjects for this study.

HOUSTON, DRUSILLA DUNJEE (author) was well-known during the Twenties for her writings on African civilization. At

that time, she had three volumes entitled Wonderful Ethiopians.
Two additional volumes were entitled Ethiopians of the New
World.

JOHNSON, GEORGIA DOUGLAS (poet, playwright, schooltea-
cher, musician) christened her home "Halfway House" and for
forty years used it as a meeting place for such "black artists
and intellectuals as Langston Hughes, Owen Dodson, Sterling
Brown, May Miller ..."

JOHNSON, JEFFALYN (public administrator, political scientist, educator psychologist, consultant) brings together her
education and experience in a number of fields to provide ex-
pertise in personal and organization development in govern-
ment and private organizations. She focuses on administrative
organizations and administrative behavior by analyzing the
structures of organizations and the roles individuals play in
order to improve their effectiveness and increase their pro-
ductivity. More specifically, Dr. Johnson applies her training and experience as a public administrator and political
scientist to working with top-level Federal career executives
in developing management systems and solving management
problems. She draws from her background as an educator
and psychologist to assist in developing effective interpersonal
relations skills and methods of integrating personal goals and
objectives with those of the organization. Dr. Johnson's primary goal is to bring about organizational changes that result
in more effective delivery of goods and services to people.

JORDAN, BARBARA (Congresswoman from Texas) "sponsored
the first piece of major legislation to pass the Texas Senate
in 1960 and also the first legislation from the Texas Legislature in 12 years to increase workers' compensation."

MASON, BIDDY (former slave, midwife, nurse, philanthropist)
opened her downtown Los Angeles home to newcomers in need
of assistance. Mrs. Mason, who also helped found the first
African Methodist Church in Los Angeles, gave great financial
assistance to white and Black churches; she visited the prisons,
and she paid the grocery bills for 1880 flood victims.

MATTHEWS, MIRRIAM (bibliographer, historian, photographer,
private collector, and retired librarian) has accumulated several thousand photographs of Blacks in California. Miss Matthews, concerned about the preservation of accurate records,
has identified most of these pictures and has written biographical sketches about some of the subjects.

MOSIKA, AMINATA (Abbey Lincoln--actress, playwright, singer) was one of four producers of a mammoth tribute to Black women, Shrine Auditorium, January, 1977.

MOTEN, ETTA (former concert singer) is one of the persons who popularized African art in the United States when she and friends promoted an Afro-Arts Bazaar in New York City.

NICKERSON, CAMMILLE (composer, concert pianist and concert singer, educator) toured the country, giving recitals which included Creole songs, many of which she had arranged and harmonized. Miss Nickerson gave great authenticity to the works when she dressed in "historic native costumes."

NORTON, ELEANOR HOLMES (former head of the New York Human Rights Commission) includes sex as one of the irrational factors sometimes causing discrimination.

PATTERSON, EDDIMARIE (historian and truth seeker) is actively involved in planning a trip to the Nile Valley in search of Black Man's ancient history, so that Black children can re-identify with their own ancient history.

POWELL, GLORIA (psychiatrist, researcher) has published a book entitled Black Monday's Children: The Effects of School Desegregation, which concludes, among other things, that integration is more difficult for Black girls than for boys--if the home life and community life of the children have not been kept intact.

SPURLOCK, JEANNE (psychiatrist) found that Black women have not been as dominant as they have been portrayed by social scientists.

TEMPLE, DR. RUTH (the first woman Graduate of Loma Linda Medical College and the first known Black woman to practice medicine in California) conceived the idea of a total health program which had four aspects: 1) The first phase of the program was a health study club which would offer health training courses and positive health action projects. 2) The second phase was a health information center strategically placed. 3) The third aspect was an inner city block-to-block plan of community work. 4) The fourth phase was a community health week--now observed in the Los Angeles area and state-wide. The purpose of the total health program is three-dimensional: "To prepare, train, and motivate people to have new faith in God, country, fellowmen, and in that faith to prevent preventable problems, such as diseases, disorders, tragedies, violence, and crime; to conserve energy and meet basic health needs; and to go forward together and reach the highest realizable goals in happiness, development, service, and in maximum total health or wholeness of body, mind, and soul." So sound and innovative is her health program that Presidents Kennedy, Johnson, and Nixon have endorsed it, commending Dr. Temple for her remarkable achievements in the field of public health education.

TERRELL, MARY CHURCH (author, champion of women's rights, educator, civil rights advocate, lecturer) was a woman of many great ideas and deeds. When invited to the International Congress of Women in Berlin, 1904, she gave her speech in fluent German, then in fluent French, and last in fluent English. Years later, using an old forgotten law that had been left on the books, she filed a discrimination suit against a number of Washington, D.C. restaurants. Her efforts resulted in ending segregation in Washington's public accommodations.

WALKER, MADAME C. J. (1869-1919) invented a hair softener and the straightening comb. She then founded a business which included assistants, agents, schools, and a manufacturing company.

WALKER, MAGGIE L. (1867-1934) originated the first-known plan by which school children could open and make regular contributions to savings accounts in the St. Luke Penny Savings Bank, Richmond, Virginia. The Virginia State Federation of Women decided to build a home, with a school and farm, for neglected girls when a judge sentenced an eight-year-old girl to jail. Some of the women who were instrumental in the establishing of the Virginia Industrial School for Colored Girls were Mrs. Maggie Walker and Mrs. Janie Barrett.

WELLS, IDA B. (teacher, journalist, lecturer, social service worker, and anti-lynching crusader) began documenting and publishing lynching incidents after Northern newspapers refused to give full or objective treatment of lynchings. Her works, Southern Horrors and A Red Record, were the first documented works on lynching. Mrs. Wells also encouraged Black women to organize. The Ida B. Wells Club, which she founded, was the first organization of Black women in Chicago. Among her convictions was that the NAACP fell short of meeting its goals because of limitations of some of the white leadership. She also led a delegation to see President McKinley about the lynching of a Black postmaster.

WELSING, FRANCES (educator, lecturer, psychiatrist) has formulated the Cress Theory, which says, in part, that the White need to feel superior to non-Whites is actually "compensation for a sense of inadequacy and inferiority."

WILLIAMS, FRANCES (actress, lecturer) insists that women and men must work together for the liberation of the oppressed third world and of all working people.

BLACK PERIODICALS

Black Academy Review. Black Academy Press, 135 University Avenue, Buffalo, New York.

Black Art: An International Quarterly. 137-55 Southgate St., Jamaica, New York 11413 (212-276-7681).

Black Lines: A Journal of Black Studies. P.O. Box 7195, Pittsburgh.

Black Scholar: Journal of Black Studies and Research. P.O. Box 908, Sausalito, Calif.

CLA Journal, Morgan State College, Baltimore, Md. 21739.

Crisis. 1970 Broadway, New York.

Dasein: The Quarterly Review. G.P.O. Box 2121, New York 10001.

Essence. Marcia Gillespie, editor. 102 E. 30th Street, New York 10016.

First World, An International Journal of Black Thought. 1580 Avon Ave., S.W. Atlanta, Georgia 30311.

Free Lance: A Magazine of Poetry and Prose. 6005 Grand Ave., Cleveland 44104.

Freedomways. 799 Broadway, Suite 544, New York 10003.

Journal of Black Poetry. 922 Haight St., Apt. B., San Francisco 94117.

The Journal of Negro History. 1538 Ninth St. N.W., Washington, D.C.

Liberator. 244 E. 46th St., New York 10017.

Muhammed Speaks.   2548 S. Federal St. , Chicago.

The Negro History Bulletin.   1538 Ninth St. N. W. , Washing-
     ton, D. C. 20001.

Neworld: A Quarterly of the Inner City Cultural Center.
     1008 South New Hampshire Ave. , Los Angeles, Califor-
     nia 90006 (213-387-1161).

Nkombo.   P. O. Box 51826, New Orleans 70150.

Nommo: The Journal of the Obac Writer's Workshop.   77 E.
     35th St. , Chicago 60616.

Our Voice.   901 College St. N. W. , Knoxville, Tenn.   37921.

Patterns: Newsletter of the Institute for Black Studies.   3026
     Wellington Road, Los Angeles 90016.

Phylon.   223 Chestnut St. S. W. , Atlanta 30314.

Présence Africaine: Revue Culturelle du Monde Noir.   24 bis
     rue des Ecoles, Paris (5e), France.

Rhythm.   859 1/2 Hunter St. N. W. , Atlanta 30314.

Soulbook.   P. O. Box 1097, Berkeley, Calif. 94701.

Tan.   1820 S. Michigan Ave. , Chicago 60616.

Theatre of Afro Arts.   P. O. Box 94, N. W. Branch, Miami,
     Fla. 33147.

Umbra.   P. O. Box 374, Peter Stuyvesant Station, New York
     10009.

Vibration.   P. O. Box 08152, Cleveland 51108.

BLACK PUBLISHING HOUSES

African World Distributors, 28-1/2 E. 33rd Street, #2A, New York 10016.

Afro-Am Publishing Company, 1727 South Indiana Ave., Chicago 60616.

Associated Publishers, 1538 19th Ave. N.W., Washington, D.C. 20001.

Black Academy Press, 135 University Ave., Buffalo, N.Y. 14214.

Black Star Publishers, 8824 Finkle Street, Detroit 48200.

Broadside Press, 12651 Old Mill Place, Detroit 48239.

Buckingham Learning Corporation, 75 Madison Avenue, New York 10016.

Drum and Spear Press, 1902 Belmont Road N.W., Washington, D.C. 20009.

Edward W. Blyden Press, P.O. Box 621, Manhattanville Station, New York 10027.

Emerson Hall Publishers Company, 209 West 97th Street, New York 10025.

Free Black Press, 7850 S. Cottage Grove Ave., Chicago 60619.

Free Lance Press, 5000 Grand Ave., Cleveland 44104.

Free Southern Theatre, 1716 N. Miro Street, New Orleans 70119.

Jihad Productions, P.O. Box 663, Newark, N.J. 07103.

Johnson Publishing Company, 1820 S. Michigan Ave., Chicago 60616.

Journal of Black Poetry Press, 922 Haight Street, Apt. B, San Francisco 94117.

Julian Richardson Associates, 540 McAllister Street, San Francisco.

Oamuru Press, Inc., 161 Madison Ave., #2A, New York 10016.

Oduduwa Productions, Inc., University of Pittsburgh, Black Studies Department, Pittsburgh 15213.

The Third Press, 444 Central Park West, New York 10025.

Third World Press, 7850 S. Ellis Ave., Chicago 60619.

Vibration Press, P.O. Box 18152, Cleveland 44108.

INDEX